God's Little Devotional Book
for Everyone

God's Little
Devotional Book
for Everyone

eagle

Guildford, Surrey

British Library Cataloguing-in-Publication Data. A catalogue record for this book is available from the British Library.

Originally published by Honor Books, Oklahoma. USA. This edition published in the UK by Eagle, an imprint of Inter Publishing Service (IPS) Ltd, St Nicholas House, 14 The Mount, Guildford, Surrey GU2 5HN.

Scripture quotations used throughout this book are as follows:
AV – *Authorised Version*
NJK – *New King James Version*, © Thomas Nelson
NIV – *New International Version*, © Hodder & Stoughton
TLB – *The Living Bible*, © Tyndale House, 1971
JBP – *J B Phillips*, © Fontana Books, 1960
GNB – *The Good News Bible*, © Bible Society
NASB – *The New American Standard Bible*, © The Lockman Foundation, 1960, 1962, 1963, 1968, 1971, 1972, 1973, 1975, 1977.
RSV – *Revised Standard Version*, © Division of Christian Education of the National Council of the Churches of Christ in the USA, 1946, 1952.

Printed in the UK by Cox & Wyman Ltd, Reading, Berkshire.

ISBN: 0 86347 234 6

Introduction

Everyone can use a little inspiration, a little reminder of what is truly good, moral and just. *God's Little Devotional Book* provides just that!

These devotionals – linked to often well known pithy quotations and also to verses from the Bible are short and easy-to-read . . . but no less meaningful. You'll find anecdotes, illustrations and stories that make you laugh, challenge you to think, and in some cases, touch the soft spot of your heart. As one reader has said, 'Some of these hit me right between the eyes . . . and others caused tears to come to my eyes.' Either way, this book promises you an expanded vision and new insights. And because the devotionals are tied to the eternal truth of God's Word, they also will help build in you excellence of character and strength of integrity.

God's Little Devotional Book is for readers of all ages, in all circumstances of life, in all professions. These devotionals are ones to which virtually every person can relate, and from which every person can draw encouragement. They'll add meaning to your day with truth, even as they brighten your day with hope! Share them with your children. Share them with a friend. They're guaranteed to offer a road map to succeed in the daily journey of life!

A marriage may be made
in heaven, but the
maintenance must
be done on earth.

*Let every one of you who is a husband
love his wife as he loves himself, and let
every wife respect her husband.*
Ephesians 5:33 (JBP)

A woman once went away on a long-weekend retreat with a group of women from her church. About halfway through the final Monday morning session, she suddenly jumped to her feet and left the room. Concerned, a friend followed her to see what had caused her to leave the meeting so abruptly. She found her friend just as she was hanging up a telephone in the lobby.

'Is everything all right?' she asked urgently.

'Oh, yes,' the woman responded. 'I didn't mean to cause you alarm.' A bit sheepishly, she added, 'I suddenly remembered that it's Monday morning – dustbin day.'

'Dustbin day? Your husband is still at home. Surely . . .'

'Yes,' the woman interrupted, 'but it takes two of us to put out the trash. I can't carry it. And he can't remember it.'

Marriages are meant to be complementary – two pulling together as one, not in competition, but in mutual association. Learning how to work together and how to live together is the 'maintenance' of love.

When God measures a man, He puts the tape around the heart instead of the head.

. . . the LORD sees not as man sees; man looks on the outward appearance, but the LORD looks on the heart.

1 Samuel 16:7 (RSV)

President Lincoln had a disarming and engaging ability to laugh at himself, especially his own physical appearance. When Senator Stephen A. Douglas once called him a 'two-faced man', Lincoln responded, 'I leave it to my audience. If I had another face, do you think I would wear this one?'

Another time he told a group of editors about meeting a woman riding on horseback in the wood. She 'looked at me intently, and said, "I do believe you are the ugliest man I ever saw." Said I, "Madam, you are probably right, but I can't help it." "No," said she, "you can't help it, but you might stay at home."'

Although his likeness is widely recognised, Lincoln is not known primarily for his appearance, but for his courageous stance for restoration of the Union and the abolition of slavery. He is often held up as an example of remarkable patience, determination, dedication, strong will, compassion, thoughtfulness and selflessness. These inner qualities are what mark Lincoln as one of America's greatest presidents.

So much is made in our culture today of outward appearance and material possessions. We do well to remember that it is our virtuous inner qualities that create a lasting reputation.

The grass may look greener on the other side, but it still has to be mowed.

. . . And be content with such things as ye have . . .
Hebrews 13:5 (AV)

A stonecutter once delivered a slab of stone to a merchant. Seeing all his wonderful goods, he said, 'I wish I was a merchant and had such things.' In the twinkling of an eye, his wish was granted. Then one day he saw a parade pass his shop window. In it he saw a prince pass by in splendour and he said, 'I wish I was a prince.' And immediately he became a prince . . . until the day the hot sun beat down upon him and he said, 'I wish I was the sun, greater than any man.' And he became the sun and was happy . . . until a cloud came between him and the earth. He said, 'That cloud overshadows me. I wish I was a cloud.' Again his wish was granted. He rained down on the earth to his heart's content until he came to a mountain, which wouldn't let him pass. He said, 'That mountain is greater than I, I wish I was a mountain.' Instantly, he became a mountain and he thought. *Now I am the greatest of all.*

But one day a little man climbed up the mountain and with a hammer and chisel began to tap away at it. The mountain, unable to stop him, said, 'That little man is greater than I, I wish I was a man who cut stone.' Once again his wish was granted and he became a stonecutter. He lived a long and useful life and everyone marvelled at how happy he was.

Patience is the ability to keep your motor idling when you feel like stripping your gears.

Better a patient man than a warrior,
a man who controls his temper than one
who takes a city.
Proverbs 16:32 (NIV)

An old train on a branch line was puffing and creaking slowly through the countryside when suddenly it lurched to a stop. The only passenger in the three-carriage train rose quickly to his feet and hurried to find the conductor. 'Why have we stopped?' he demanded. 'I'm a salesman and I have an appointment in less than an hour in the next town. Surely this old train can make it through a pasture!'

The conductor smiled. 'Nothing to worry about, sir. Just a cow on the tracks. Gotta wait her out.' The salesman returned to his seat, fuming and fidgeting until the train began to creep forwards again about ten minutes later. It chugged along for a mile or two and then ground to a halt once again.

This time the conductor found the salesman. 'Don't worry,' he said. 'We'll be on our way shortly. It's just a temporary delay.' The exasperated salesman asked. 'What now? Did we catch up with the cow again?'

What the salesman didn't know was that the schedule for this particular train had been made so as to *allow* for temporary delays and cows on the track! The salesman made his appointment on time but he was worn to a frazzle by his own frustration and concern.

Allow for delays. You'll enjoy life's journey more.

He who is waiting for something to turn up might start with his own shirt sleeves.

All hard work brings a profit,
but mere talk leads only to poverty.
Proverbs 14:23 (NIV)

Many people remember President Theodore Roosevelt as an avid hunter and sportsman. Few, however, know of his efforts for conservation, which is a far greater legacy.

After a hunting trip to the Dakota region in 1887 – years before he was president – Roosevelt returned to his East Coast home reporting that trees were being cut down carelessly, animals were being slaughtered by 'swinish game-butchers', and that the wilderness was in danger. He expressed great shock at how quickly the region that he loved was being stripped of its glory – the big game gone, the ponds drying up, the beavers disappearing, the grasslands becoming desert.

But Roosevelt did more than talk. He founded the Boone & Crockett Club, dedicated to the preservation of wilderness in America. Largely through that club's influence, legislation was passed to care for Yellowstone National Park, to protect sequoia trees in California, to set aside nature reserves for bird and sea life, and to limit the shooting of big game. Laws were passed to regulate hunting practices.

Hoping for change rarely brings about change. Work, however, generally does!

Remember the banana –
when it left the bunch, it got
skinned.

*Let us not give up meeting together, as
some are in the habit of doing, but let us
encourage one another – and all the more
as you see the Day approaching.*
Hebrews 10:25 (NIV)

Few sights evoke as much attention, and awe, as that of a large flock of Canadian geese winging their way in their V-formation to the North or South. They speak of the changing of seasons, and also of the value of teamwork.

What many don't know is that when a goose gets sick, or perhaps is wounded by a shot, it never falls from formation by itself. Two other geese also fall out of formation with it and follow the ailing goose down to the ground. One of them is very often the mate of the wounded bird, since geese mate for life and are extremely loyal to their mates. Once on the ground, the healthy birds help protect him and care for him as much as possible, even to the point of throwing themselves between the weakened bird and possible predators. They stay with him until he is either able to fly or until he is dead. Then, and only then, do they launch out on their own. In most cases, they wait for another group of geese to fly overhead and they join them, adding to the safety and flying efficiency of their members.

If only we human beings would care for one another this well! Stick with your friends . . . and more importantly, stick by them.

It is better to be silent
and be considered a fool
than to speak
and remove all doubt.

Even when the fool walks on the road,
he lacks sense,
and he says to everyone
that he is a fool.
Ecclesiastes 10:3 (RSV)

William Penn, leader of the early American colonists who eventually named their state of Pennsylvania in his honour, gave these rules regarding conversation:

- 'Avoid company where it is not profitable or necessary, and in those occasions, speak little, and last.

- Silence is wisdom where speaking is folly, and always safe.

- Some are so foolish as to interrupt and anticipate those that speak instead of hearing and thinking before they answer. Which is uncivil, as well as silly.

- If thou thinkest twice before thou speakest once, thou wilt speak twice the better for it.

- Better to say nothing than not to the purpose. And to speak pertinently, consider both what is fit, and when it is fit, to speak.

- In all debates, let truth be thy aim, not victory or an unjust interest; and endeavour to gain, rather than to expose, thy antagonist.'

Many a good man has failed because he had his wishbone where his backbone should have been.

Have not I commanded you? Be strong and of good courage; do not be afraid, nor be dismayed, for the LORD your God is with you wherever you go.
Joshua 1:9 (NKJ)

At one point during his youth, baseball great Jackie Robinson began to run with a neighbourhood gang. In later years, he recalled that while he had *wished* for a better life as a boy and teen, he had no understanding that a gang was not the way to achieve it. An older friend finally came to Jackie and made him realise how much he was hurting his hard-working mother, as well as how much he was limiting himself. Robinson said, 'He told me that it didn't take guts to follow the crowd, that courage and intelligence lay in being willing to be different.'

Jackie listened, left the gang, and traded his wishbone for a backbone. He began to work on developing his own physical potential and within a few short years, became a sensational athlete. Starring in football, basketball, baseball and track at UCLA, he was the first person to win athletic awards in all four sports at the university. He went on to play professional football with the Los Angeles Bulldogs before being drafted for World War II duty. After the war, he signed with the Brooklyn Dodgers. Not only did Jackie Robinson become the first black baseball player in the major leagues, but he was voted rookie of the year.

Backbone accomplishes more than wishbone!

If at first you don't succeed, try reading the instructions.

Hold on to instruction, do not let it go;
guard it well, for it is your life.
Proverbs 4:13 (NIV)

A young ensign had nearly completed his first overseas tour of sea duty when he was given an opportunity to display his ability at getting the ship under way. With a stream of crisp commands, he had the decks buzzing with men and soon the ship had left port and was steaming out of the channel.

The ensign's efficiency had been remarkable. In fact, the deck was abuzz with talk that he had set a new record for getting a destroyer under way. The ensign glowed at his accomplishment and was not all that surprised when another seaman approached him with a message from the captain. He was, however, a bit surprised to find that it was a *radio* message, and he was even more surprised when he read, 'My personal congratulations upon completing your underway preparation exercise according to the book and with amazing speed. In your haste, however, you have overlooked one of the unwritten rules – make sure the captain is aboard before getting under way.'

God's Manual for Life, the Bible, is our 'set of instructions' for getting our lives under way. But we must never become so bound to the book that we forget the Author of it and the relationship He wishes to have with us on the voyage.

Your temper is like a fire. It gets very destructive when it gets out of control.

Whoever has no rule over his own spirit
Is like a city broken down, without walls.
Proverbs 25:28 (NKJ)

When a person loses his temper, one of the most common expressions used to describe the situation is to 'fly off the handle'. This phrase refers to the head of a hammer coming loose from its handle as the carpenter attempts to use it. Several things happen as a result.

First, the hammer becomes useless – no longer good for work. In like manner, when a person loses his temper, he often loses his effectiveness. Anything he says may not be taken seriously and is likely to be unproductive.

Second, the hammerhead – twirling out of control – is likely to cause some type of damage to anything in its path. The person who loses his temper causes damage even if he doesn't realise it – perhaps physically to people or objects in his way, and nearly always emotionally to those who feel they are victims of uncontrolled wrath.

Third, the repair of both the hammer and the resulting damage takes time. The person who loses his temper may recover quickly, but the other one who is the victim of a hot temper rarely recovers as quickly.

Keep your temper today. Nobody else wants it.

Decisions can take you out of God's will but never out of His reach.

If we are faithless, he will remain faithful, for he cannot disown himself.
2 Timothy 2:13 (NIV)

In her book, *A Closer Walk*, author Catherine Marshall tells about a great personal struggle she experienced after writing a novel titled *Gloria*. Marshall began the novel in 1969 and then abandoned the project two-and-a-half years later. To her, the shelved manuscript was 'like a death in the family'.

In attempting to reconcile her conflicting thoughts and feelings, Marshall spent time in a retreat house in Florida. While there, she reread a Bible story from Numbers about a time when poisonous snakes filled the Israelite camp. The people recognised the snakes as a punishment for their sin, and cried out in repentance. The Lord told Moses to 'make a [bronze] snake and put it up on a pole. Then when anyone was bitten by a snake and looked at the bronze snake, he lived' (Numbers 21:9 NIV).

Catherine Marshall realised that just as the Israelites took that which had hurt them, lifted it up to God, and were healed, so we each can take our mistakes and sins, lift them to God in prayer, and trust Him to heal us. She writes, 'When any one of us has made a wrong (or even doubtful) turning in our lives through arrogance or lack of trust or impatience or fear – God will show us a way out.' Even when we stray, He knows both where we are and how to get us back on His path.

Your companions are like
the buttons on an elevator.
They will either take you up
or they will take you down.

He who walks with wise men will be wise,
But the companion of fools will be
destroyed.
Proverbs 13:20 (NKJ)

A scorpion, being a very poor swimmer, once asked a turtle to carry him on his back across a river. 'Are you mad?' exclaimed the turtle. 'You'll sting me while I'm swimming and I'll drown.'

The scorpion laughed as he replied, 'My dear turtle, if I were to sting you, you would drown and I would go down with you. Now, what would be the point of that? I won't sting you. It would mean my own death!'

The turtle thought about the logic of his argument for a few moments and then said, 'You're right. Hop on!' The scorpion climbed aboard and halfway across the river, he gave the turtle a mighty sting.

As the turtle began to sink to the bottom of the river with the scorpion on its back, it moaned in dismay, 'After your promise, you stung me! Why did you do that? Now, we're both doomed.'

The drowning scorpion sadly replied, 'I couldn't help it. It's my nature to sting.'

Study the character of a person before you make them a friend. The stage on which their character plays is going to be your life!

Patience is a quality you admire in the driver behind you and scorn in the one ahead.

The end of a matter is better
than its beginning,
and patience is better than pride.
Do not be quickly provoked in your spirit,
for anger resides in the lap of fools.
Ecclesiastes 7:8,9 (NIV)

A man's car once stalled in heavy Friday evening traffic just as the light turned green. All his efforts to start the engine failed. A chorus of honking rose from the cars behind him.

Feeling just as frustrated as those other drivers eager to get home or to their weekend destinations, he finally got out of his car and walked back to the first driver and said, 'I'm sorry, but I can't seem to get my car started. If you'll go up there and give it a try, I'll stay here and blow your horn for you.'

The person who is chronically impatient rarely makes another person go faster or arrive earlier. Rather, the effects are nearly always negative – to others as well as to the impatient person. Accidents occur more frequently in haste. Ulcers, headaches and other health problems develop more quickly. And relationships can become more readily strained.

As an antidote for impatience, try giving yourself 'ten more minutes'. Get up ten minutes earlier every morning, leave ten minutes earlier, arrive ten minutes ahead of schedule, and so forth. You'll probably arrive at the end of the day feeling much more relaxed.

There is a name for people who are not excited about their work – unemployed.

And whatever you do, do it heartily, as to the Lord and not to men.
Colossians 3:23 (NKJ)

Thomas Edison, who held 1,093 patents for his inventions – which include the light bulb, phonograph, and motion-picture camera, sold the rights to many of his inventions to Western Union and other large companies to keep his workshop going. Over time, others made far more money from Edison's inventions than he did, but this didn't seem to bother him a great deal. He once said, 'I don't care so much about making my fortune as I do for getting ahead of the other fellow.' Edison's greatest desire was to be both the first and the best in his field, to out-invent everybody he could. He worked tirelessly, with joy.

Edison eventually established Menlo Park, the world's first factory for the making of nothing but inventions. It was a forerunner of the private research laboratories now maintained by many large companies. At Menlo Park, Edison promised to turn out 'a minor invention every ten days and a big thing every six months or so'. At one point, he was working on forty-seven new things at once.

Other inventors may have been richer than Edison, but virtually no inventor has ever been more enthusiastic or more successful. For him, enthusiasm and employment were inextricably bound together!

A person's true character is revealed by what he does when no one is watching.

Obey them not only to win their favour when their eye is on you, but like slaves of Christ, doing the will of God from your heart.
Ephesians 6:6 (NIV)

Ted Engstrom tells the following story in his book titled *Integrity*:

'For Coach Cleveland Stroud and the Bulldogs of Rockdale County High School (Conyers, Georgia), it was their championship season: 21 wins and 5 losses on the way to the Georgia boys' basketball tournament last March, then a dramatic come-from-behind victory in their state finals.

'But now the new glass trophy case outside the school gymnasium is bare. Earlier this month the Georgia High School Association deprived Rockdale County of the championship after school officials said that a player who was scholastically ineligible had played 45 seconds in the first of the school's five postseason games.

' "We didn't know he was ineligible at the time; we didn't know it until a few weeks ago," Mr Stroud said. "Some people have said we should have just kept quiet about it, that it was just 45 seconds and the player wasn't an impact player. But you've got to do what's honest and right and what the rules say. I told my team that people forget the scores of basketball games; they don't ever forget what you're made of." '

It's better to die with a good
name than to live with a
bad one.

*A good name is better than
precious ointment.*
Ecclesiastes 7:1 (AV)

A man once went to his solicitor and made this request: 'I am going into a business deal with a man I do not trust. I want you to frame an airtight contract that he can't break, and which will protect me from any sort of mischief he may have on his mind.'

The solicitor replied: 'Frankly, there's no group of words in the English language that can take the place of plain honesty between men. There's nothing that can be put into a contract that will *fully* protect either of you if one of you *plans* to deceive the other.'

Your name is tied to your character. If your character is bad so will be your name. You are wise to establish a reputation for having a good name, a reputation for being honest, trustworthy and steadfast. Your name will not only follow you all the days of your life but all the days of your children's lives as well.

Before entering into a business deal or employment relationship, ask yourself:

1. How has this person treated others? Talk to his former associates, clients, vendors and former employees.

2. How does this person talk about business? Does he brag about destroying others, or winning by shrewdness? If so, you are probably dealing with a scheming person who attempts to 'use' people.

Work with those who have sterling reputations. Your own reputation is less likely to become tarnished.

'No' is one of the few words that can never be misunderstood.

But let your statement be 'yes, yes'
or 'no, no'. . .
Matthew 5:37 (NASB)

Although taken captive as children, Hananiah, Mishael and Azariah were so wise that as adults they were put over the affairs of the Babylon province. Then the king they served built a gold image some 100 feet high and placed it in their province. He invited the empire's leaders to a dedication of the image and gave a command that when a tribute of music was sounded, all should fall and worship the golden image. Whoever didn't do so would be thrown into a giant furnace.

The music played, and all fell on their faces . . . except Hananiah, Mishael and Azariah. They were Jews, and had been taught from earliest memory never to worship a graven image. Word of their refusal quickly came to the king, and in a rage he summoned them. The three leaders didn't hesitate in saying to the king, 'We will not serve your gods, nor worship the golden image' (Daniel 3:18).

Furious, the king had the three cast into the fire, only to find that they did not burn. They emerged unscorched! The 'no' of these faithful men resulted in the king decreeing that no person in the land speak anything against their God. And Hananiah, Mishael and Azariah – whom the king called Shadrach, Meshach and Abed-Nego – were promoted.

If your answer is 'no' than make it mean something. When you stand by your word God will stand by you.

Too many churchgoers are singing 'Standing on the Promises' when all they are doing is sitting on the premises.

We do not want you to become lazy, but to be like those who believe and are patient, and so receive what God has promised.
Hebrews 6:12 (GNB)

The story is told of a lazy boy who went with his mother and aunt on a blueberry-picking hike into the woods. He carried the smallest pail possible. While the others worked hard at picking berries, he lolled about, chasing a butterfly and playing hide and seek with a squirrel. Soon it was approaching time to leave. In a panic, he filled his pail mostly with moss and then topped it off with a thick layer of berries, so that the pail looked full of berries. His mother and aunt commended him highly for his effort.

The next morning his mother baked pies, and she made a special 'saucer-sized' pie just for the boy. He could hardly wait for it to cool. Blueberry pie was his favourite! He could see the plump berries oozing through a slit in the crust, and his mouth watered in anticipation. However, as he sunk his fork into the flaky crust, he found . . . mostly moss!

Many people want to experience the fullness of God's promises in their lives, but they are unwilling to do the work that goes along with most of the Bible's promises. Most of God's promises are if-then statements . . . if we do one thing, God will do another. Our part nearly always comes first!

Some people complain
because God put thorns on
roses, while others praise
Him for putting roses
among thorns.

Finally, brethren, whatever things are
true, whatever things are noble, whatever
things are just, whatever things are pure,
whatever things are lovely, whatever
things are of good report, if there is any
virtue and if there is anything
praiseworthy – meditate on these things.
Philippians 4:8 (NKJ)

The pessimist will see a glass filled to the halfway mark with water as being half empty, the optimist as being half full. And the optimistically *creative* person will see it as a vase for a rosebud, the optimistic *pragmatist* as a means of quenching thirst, the optimistic *priest* as water to bless for baptism!

Consider the benefits of choosing the optimistic route as described in this poem:

Two frogs fell into a deep cream bowl,
One was an optimistic soul;
But the other took the gloomy view,
'I shall drown,' he cried, 'and so will you.'
So with a last despairing cry,
He closed his eyes and said, 'Good-bye.'
But the other frog, with a merry grin
Said, 'I can't get out, but I won't give in!
I'll swim around till my strength is spent.
For having tried, I'll die content.'
Bravely he swam until it would seem
His struggles began to churn the cream.
On the top of the butter at last he stopped
And out of the bowl he happily hopped.
What is the moral? It's easily found.
If you can't get out – keep swimming around!

The cure of crime is not in the electric chair, but in the high chair.

Train up a child in the way he should go: And when he is old, he will not depart from it.
Proverbs 22:6 (AV)

The importance of the first few years of a child's life cannot be overestimated. It is during those years that the foundation is laid for a child's language ability, ethics, morality and value systems. In his book, *All Men Are Brothers*, Mahatma Gandhi said this about the instilling of values in very early childhood: 'I am convinced that for the proper upbringing of children the parents ought to have a general knowledge of the care and nursing of babies . . . We labour under a sort of superstition that the child has nothing to learn during the first five years of its life. On the contrary the fact is that the child never learns in later life what it does in its first five years. The education of the child begins with conception.'

The famous psychoanalyst Sigmund Freud agreed. A Viennese woman once asked him, 'How early should I begin the education of my child?'

Freud replied with a question of his own, 'When will your child be born?'

'Born?' the woman asked, 'Why he is already five years old!'

'My goodness woman,' Freud cried, 'don't stand there talking to me – hurry home! You have already wasted the five best years!'

The bridge you burn now
may be one you later have
to cross.

*Do everything possible on your part to live
in peace with everybody.*
Romans 12:18 (GNB)

When Abraham Lincoln was campaigning for the presidency, one of his arch-enemies was Edwin McMasters Stanton. Stanton hated Lincoln, and used every ounce of his energy to degrade Lincoln in the eyes of the public, often using the bitterest diatribes in an attempt to embarrass him.

In the process of choosing his cabinet after his election, Lincoln selected various members and then faced a decision about the important post of Secretary of War. He chose Stanton! The president's inner circle erupted in an uproar when they heard his choice. Numerous advisors came to Lincoln saying, 'Mr President, you are making a mistake. Are you familiar with all the ugly things he has said about you? He is your enemy. He will sabotage your programmes.'

Lincoln replied, 'Yes, I know Mr Stanton. But . . . I find he is the best man for the job.'

As Secretary of War, Stanton gave invaluable service to his nation and his president. After Lincoln was assassinated, many laudable statements were made about Abraham Lincoln, but the words of Stanton remain among the greatest. Standing near Lincoln's coffin, Stanton called Lincoln one of the greatest men who ever lived and said, 'He now belongs to the ages.'

The measure of a man is
not how great his faith is,
but how great his love is.

And now these three remain:
faith, hope and love.
But the greatest of these is love.
1 Corinthians 13:13 (NIV)

In 1873, a Belgian Catholic priest named Joseph Damien De Veuster was sent to minister to lepers on the Hawaiian island of Molokai. He arrived in high spirits, hoping to build a friendship with each of the lepers. People shunned him, however, at every turn. He built a chapel, began worship services, poured his heart out to the lepers, but all seemed futile. No one responded to his ministry and after twelve years of struggling, Father Damien decided to leave. As he stood in dejection on the dock waiting to board ship, he looked down at the hands he was wringing and noticed some mysterious white spots on them. Feeling some numbness, he knew immediately what was happening – he had contracted leprosy!

Father Damien returned to the leper colony and to his work. Word spread quickly and within hours, hundreds gathered outside his hut, fully identifying with his plight. A bigger surprise came the following Sunday. When he arrived at the chapel, he found it full! Father Damien began to preach from the empathy of love rather than the distance of theology and ideas, and his ministry became enormously successful.

Those who receive your love today will be much more interested in hearing about your faith tomorrow.

Real friends are those who,
when you've made a fool of
yourself, don't feel you've
done a permanent job.

Love bears all things, believes all things,
hopes all things, endures all things. Love
never ends . . .
1 Corinthians 13:7,8 (RSV)

One of the most notable friendships in literature is that which Melanie has with Scarlett O'Hara in Margaret Mitchell's classic, *Gone With The Wind*. Melanie is characterised as a woman who 'always saw the best in everyone and remarked kindly upon it'. Even when Scarlett tries to confess her shameful behaviour toward Ashley, Melanie's husband, Melanie says, 'Darling, I don't want any explanation . . . Do you think I could remember you walking in a furrow behind that Yankee's horse almost barefooted and with your hands blistered – just so the baby and I could have something to eat – and then believe such dreadful things about you? I don't want to hear a word.'

Melanie's refusal to believe ill of Scarlett leads Scarlett passionately to desire to 'keep Melanie's high opinion. She only knew that she did not care what the world thought of her or what Ashley or Rhett thought of her, but Melanie must not think her other than she had always thought her.'

It is as Melanie lies dying that Scarlett faces her deep need for Melanie's pure and generous friendship: 'Panic clutching at her heart, she knew that Melanie had been her sword and her shield, her comfort and her strength.' In two words, Melanie had been her *true friend*.

Be careful that your marriage doesn't become a duel instead of a duet.

Let us then pursue what makes for peace and for mutual upbuilding.
Romans 14:19 (RSV)

Newspaper columnist and minister George Crane tells of a wife who came to his office full of hatred towards her husband. Fully intending to divorce him, she said, 'Before I divorce him, I want to hurt him as much as he has me.'

Crane advised her to go home and act as if she really loved her husband. 'Tell him how much he means to you,' he said. 'Praise him for every decent trait. Go out of your way to be as kind, considerate and generous as possible. Spare no efforts to please him, to enjoy him. Make him believe you love him . . . then drop the bomb . . . That will really hurt him.'

The woman exclaimed, 'Beautiful!' And she did as he had suggested . . . with enthusiasm, acting 'as if' she loved him. Two months later she returned to Crane, who asked 'Are you ready now to go through with the divorce?'

'Divorce!' she said. 'Never! I discovered I really do love him!'

Actions can change feelings. Motion can result in emotion. Love is established not so much by fervent promise as by often-repeated deeds.

The mighty oak was once a little nut that stood its ground.

A man shall not be established by wickedness:
But the root of the righteous shall not be moved.
Proverbs 12:3 (AV)

In the 1960s, drug companies were presenting nearly 700 applications a year to the Federal Drug Administration for new medicines. The beleaguered New Drug Section only had sixty days to review each drug before giving approval or requesting more data.

A few months after Dr Frances Kelsey joined the FDA, an established pharmaceutical firm in Ohio applied for a license to market a new drug, Kevadon. In liquid form, the drug seemed to relieve nausea in early pregnancy. It was given to millions of expectant women, mostly in Europe, Asia and Africa. Although scientific studies revealed harmful side effects, the pharmaceutical firm printed 66,957 leaflets declaring its safety. The company exerted great pressure on Dr Kelsey to give permission for labels to be printed, in anticipation of the drug's approval.

Dr Kelsey reviewed the data and said no. Through several rounds of applications, she continued to find the data 'unsatisfactory'. After a fourteen-month struggle, the company humbly withdrew its application. 'Kevadon' was thalidomide, and by that time, the horror of thalidomide deformities was becoming well publicised! One firm 'no' decision by Dr Kelsey spared untold agony in the United States.

Sometimes standing your ground on something may not seem that important but in time you may see the 'big' picture.

The secret of achievement
is to not let what
you're doing get to you
before you get to it.

Commit your works to the Lord,
And your thoughts will be established.
Proverbs 16:3 (NKJ)

Jane was only seven years old when she visited a shabby street in a nearby town, and seeing ragged children there, announced that she wanted to build a big house so that poor children would have a place to play. As a young adult, Jane and a friend, Ellen Starr, visited Toynbee Hall in London, where they saw educated people helping the poor by living among them. She and Ellen returned to the slums of Chicago, restored the old Hull mansion, and moved in! There they cared for children of working mothers, and held sewing and cooking classes. Older boys and girls had clubs at the mansion. An art gallery, playground, and public music, reading and craft rooms were created in the mansion. Her childhood dream came true!

Jane fought against child labour laws, and campaigned for adult education, day nurseries, better housing and women's suffrage. She eventually was awarded an honorary degree from Yale, was called 'America's most useful citizen' by President Theodore Roosevelt, and was given the Nobel Prize for Peace.

No matter how famous she became, however, Jane Addams remained a resident of Hull House. She died a resident of Halsted Street in the heart of the slums she had come to call home.

Most people wish to serve
God – but only in an
advisory capacity.

*Humble yourselves therefore under the
mighty hand of God, that he may exalt
you in due time.*
1 Peter 5:6 (AV)

An old poem tells of a woman who was walking through a meadow one day. As she strolled along, meditating on nature, she came upon a field of golden pumpkins. In the corner of the field stood a majestic, huge oak tree.

The woman sat under the oak tree and began musing about the strange twists in nature. Why tiny acorns on huge branches and huge pumpkins on tiny vines? She thought, *God blundered with Creation! He should have put the small acorns on the tiny vines and the large pumpkins on the huge branches.*

Before long, the woman dozed off in the warmth of the late autumn sunshine. She was awakened when a tiny acorn bounced off her nose. Chuckling to herself, she amended her previous thinking, *Maybe God was right after all!*

In every situation, God knows far more about the people and circumstances involved than we can ever know. He alone sees the beginning from the ending. He alone knows how to create a Master Plan that provides for the good of *all* those who serve Him.

Conscience is God's built-in warning system. Be very happy when it hurts you. Be very worried when it doesn't.

And so I do my best always to have a clear conscience before God and man.
Acts 24:16 (GNB)

These lines from Dr Arnot give an interesting description of a person's conscience: 'A man may be saved from death by seeing the reflection of danger in a mirror, when the danger itself could not be directly seen. The executioner with his weapon is stealthily approaching through a corridor of the castle to the spot where the devoted invalid reclines. In his musings, the captive has turned his vacant eye towards a mirror on the wall; and the faithful witness reveals the impending stroke in time to secure the escape of the victim. It is thus that the mirror in a man's breast has become in a sense the man's saviour, by revealing the wrath to come before its coming. Happy they who take the warning, happy they who turn and live!'

It has been said that man's conscience was given to him after the Fall in the Garden of Eden. Man's desire to know good and evil had been granted. But God, in His mercy, gave man a means telling good *from* evil. That mechanism, which he placed in man's heart was the conscience. Don't ignore the prompting of your conscience or let your conscience become callused. It's more than a sixth sense. It's a beacon whose homing signal is Heaven.

Most men forget God all day
and ask Him to remember
them at night.

Evening, and morning, and at noon, will I
pray, and cry aloud:
and he shall hear my voice.
Psalm 55:17 (AV)

Many people revere Francis of Assisi, the thirteenth-century saint known for his very simple lifestyle and deep love of the poor. He founded the Franciscan order, restored numerous dilapidated Italian chapels, and helped countless needy people.

What most people don't know, however, is that Francis spent most of his life not in doing good work, but in prayer. St Bonaventure wrote about him. 'Whether walking or sitting, within doors or without, at toil or at leisure, he was so absorbed in prayer that he seemed to have devoted not only his whole heart and body, but also his whole heart and time.' Francis regularly set aside hours throughout the day which he called 'appointments with God', and he never missed one, even though he had serious eye, stomach, spleen and liver problems. On one occasion, as Francis travelled through the large town of Borgo on a donkey, people pressed in upon him from all sides to touch his garments. Francis was so absorbed in prayer that when he arrived at his destination some time later, he asked when they were going to get to Borgo!

No matter how busy we are, we must never become too busy to pray. It is our prayer life that gives lasting meaning to everything else we undertake.

If you don't stand for something you'll fall for anything!

. . . If you do not stand firm in your faith, you will not stand at all.

Isaiah 7:9 (NIV)

As legend has it, a just and good man went to Sodom one day, hoping to save the city from God's judgement. He tried talking to first one individual and then the next, but nobody would engage in conversation with him.

Next, he tried carrying a picket sign that had 'Repent' written on it in large letters. Nobody paid any attention to his sign after an initial glance.

Finally he began going from street to street and from marketplace to marketplace, shouting loudly, 'Men and women, repent! What you are doing is wrong. It will kill you! It will destroy you!'

The people laughed at him, but still he went about shouting. One day, a person stopped him and said, 'Stranger, can't you see that your shouting is useless?' The man replied, 'Yes, I see that.' The person then asked, 'So why do you continue?'

The man said, 'When I arrived in this city, I was convinced that I could change them. Now I continue shouting because I don't want them to change me.'

Speak out for those things you believe to be true and good. If you remain silent, others may take your silence as agreement for their position – which may not be at all what you believe.

The measure of a man's character is not what he gets from his ancestors, but what he leaves his descendants.

A good man leaves an inheritance to his children's children:
But the wealth of the sinner is stored up for the righteous.
Proverbs 13:22 (NKJ)

If I can throw a single ray of light across the darkened pathway of another; if I can aid some soul to clearer sight of life and duty, and thus bless my brother; if I can wipe from any human cheek a tear, I shall not have lived my life in vain while here.

'If I can guide some erring one to truth, inspire within his heart a sense of duty; if I can plant within my soul of rosy youth a sense of right, a love of truth and beauty; if I can teach one man that God and heaven are near, I shall not have lived in vain while here.

'If from my mind I banish doubt and fear, and keep my life attuned to love and kindness; if I can scatter light and hope and cheer, and help remove the curse of mental blindness; if I can make more joy, more hope, less pain, I shall not have lived and loved in vain.

'If by life's roadside I can plant a tree, beneath whose shade some wearied head may rest, though I may never share its beauty, I shall yet be truly blest – though no one knows my name, nor drops a flower upon my grave, I shall not have lived in vain while here.' – *Anonymous*

Although the tongue weighs very little, few people are able to hold it.

So the tongue is a little member and boasts of great things. How great a forest is set ablaze by a small fire!
James 3:5 (RSV)

Ida and David both wanted all their sons to graduate from college. They knew their boys would have to pay their own way since David never made more than $150 a month. Still, they encouraged their sons to achieve all they could. Arthur, however, went direct from high school to a job. Edgar began studying law. When Dwight graduated, he didn't have a goal in mind, so he and Ed made a pact: Dwight would work two years while Ed studied, sending Ed as much as he could, and then they would reverse the arrangement. While working, Dwight found an opportunity that appealed to him more than college – West Point.

Both Ida and David were crushed at Dwight's decision. Ida was deeply convinced that soldiering was wicked. Still, all she ever said to him was, 'It is your choice'. David also remained silent, allowing his adult son full freedom to forge his own adult future. Yes, Ida and David wisely held their tongues – but they never withheld their applause, especially on the day their son, *General* Dwight Eisenhower, became President of the United States of America.

Refraining from giving advice may actually turn out to be the best gift you may ever give a person.

You should never let adversity get you down – except on your knees.

Is any one of you in trouble?
He should pray . . .
James 5:13 (NIV)

A young soldier fighting in Italy during World War II managed to jump into a foxhole just ahead of a spray of bullets. He immediately attempted to deepen the hole for more protection. As he was frantically scraping at the dirt with his hands, he unearthed a silver crucifix, obviously left by a previous occupant of the foxhole. A moment later, a leaping figure landed beside him as shells screamed overhead. The soldier turned to see that his new companion was an army chaplain. Holding up the crucifix, the soldier cried, 'Am I glad to see you! How do you work this thing?'

On a more serious note, Captain Eddie Rickenbacker wrote about his World War II experience. While flying on a special mission to the Pacific Islands, his plane crashed. He and his crew were lost at sea for twenty-one days before being rescued. He said, 'In the beginning many of the men were atheists or agnostics, but at the end of the terrible ordeal each, in his own way, had discovered God. Each man found salvation and strength in prayer, and a community of feeling developed which created a liveliness of human fellowship and worship, and a sense of gentle peace.'

Are you facing a problem today? Start the search for its solution with prayer.

He who wants milk should not sit on a stool in the middle of the pasture expecting the cow to back up to him.

Being lazy will make you poor, but hard work will make you rich.
Proverbs 10:4 (GNB)

Miss Jones, an elderly spinster, was the oldest resident of her Midwestern town on the day she died. In writing her obituary, the editor of the local paper became stumped after noting her age. Miss Jones had never spent a night in jail or been seen intoxicated on the streets. She also had never done anything noteworthy. While musing about what he might write, the editor went out for coffee and in the local café, he met the owner of the tombstone company, who was equally perplexed as to what to write about Miss Jones.

The editor returned to his office and assigned both the obituary and tombstone epitaph to the first reporter he saw, who happened to be the sports editor. If you pass through that little town, you'll find this on Miss Jones' tombstone:

> Here lies the bones of Nancy Jones
> For her life held no terrors.
> She lived an old maid. She died an old maid.
> No hits, no runs, no errors.

If we don't try, we don't do . . . if we don't do . . . we can't bless others. We each have a contribution to make to the lives of others. Give your best effort today. It's your best shot at scoring in the game of life.

The best bridge between hope and despair is often a good night's sleep.

*It is in vain that you rise up early
and go late to rest,
eating the bread of anxious toil;
for he gives to his beloved sleep.*
Psalm 127:2 (RSV)

When the call came from Steve Early, President Roosevelt's press secretary, Harry Truman responded immediately. He arrived only minutes later at the front door of the White House, stopping only to pick up his hat, but leaving his Secret Service escort behind. He was ushered directly to Mrs Roosevelt's suite, where the First Lady rose to greet him, then put her arm around his shoulder and said, 'The President is dead.'

This was the first inkling that Truman had of the seriousness of Franklin Roosevelt's condition. He asked if he could do anything for Mrs Roosevelt and the family, and she replied by asking him if there was anything they could do for him. Truman then went to the Oval Office and called his wife Bess, who relayed to daughter Margaret what had happened. They both came quickly to the White House and by seven o'clock that evening, Harry Truman had been sworn into office. The family went home and as was later noted in Truman's diary, '[The neighbours] gave us something to eat. I had not had anything to eat since noon. Went to bed, went to sleep, and did not worry any more.'

The next morning, he went to the Oval Office and began to master the job he always liked to say was the greatest in the world.

It is good to remember that the tea kettle, although up to its neck in hot water, continues to sing.

Rejoice evermore . . . In everything give thanks: for this is the will of God in Christ Jesus concerning you.
1 Thessalonians 5:16,18 (AV)

An old legend tells how a man once stumbled upon a great red barn after wandering for days in a dark, overgrown forest. Seeking refuge from the howling winds of a storm that seemed to rage perpetually in the forest, he let his eyes grow accustomed to the dark and then, to his astonishment, he discovered that this was the barn where Satan kept his storehouse of seeds to be sown into human hearts. More curious than fearful, he lit a match and began to explore the piles and bins of seeds around him. He couldn't help but notice that the containers labelled 'seeds of discouragement' far outnumbered any other type of seed.

Just as the man had drawn this conclusion, one of Satan's foremost demons arrived to pick up a fresh supply of seed. The man asked him why there was such an abundance of discouragement seeds. The demon laughed, 'Because they are so effective and they take root so quickly!' The man then asked, 'Do they grow everywhere?' At this the demon became sullen. He glared at the man and admitted in disgust, 'No. They never seem to thrive in the heart of a grateful person'.

Be thankful for what you have, today. And trust the Lord to take care of what you *don't* have.

It is good to be a Christian
and know it, but it's better
to be a Christian
and show it!

*By this all men will know that you are my
disciples, if you have love for one another.*
John 13:35 (RSV)

In *Les Miserables*, Victor Hugo tells of Jean Valjean, whose only crime was the theft of a loaf of bread to feed his sister's starving children. Valjean served nineteen years for his crime before being turned out penniless on the streets. Hardened and, as a former convict, unable to find work, Valjean finally makes his way to the home of a good old bishop, who gives him supper and a bed for the night. He serves Valjean using his best silver platters and candlesticks, which Valjean recognises as being highly valuable.

Yielding to temptation, Valjean steals the bishop's silver plates and slips away from the bishop's home, but is soon caught and returned by watchful police. When shown the silver plates, the bishop says to the apprehending policeman, 'Why, I gave them to him.' And then turning to the thief Valjean, he adds, 'And Jean, you forgot to take the candlesticks.' A shocked and eternally grateful Valjean accepts the candlesticks as more than valuable silver pieces, but as expressions of love beyond measure. The bishop's act brought about a true repentance and changed life.

Who knows which person might be impacted by your act of kindness today? What seems little to you may be great in the eyes of a person in need of love.

Sorrow looks back.
Worry looks around.
Faith looks up.

Fixing our eyes on Jesus, the author and perfector of faith, who for the joy set before Him endured the cross, despising the shame, and has sat down at the right hand of the throne of God.

Hebrews 12:2 (NASB)

In *Love and Duty*, Anne Purcell writes about seeing Major Jim Statler standing with her pastor outside his study after a Sunday service. She knew instantly that he was there with news about her husband, Ben, on active duty in Vietnam. As she had feared, Jim gave her a chilling message: 'He was on a helicopter that was shot down . . . he's missing in action.'

Anne recalls, 'Somewhere in the back of my mind, a little candle flame flickered. This tiny flame was the vestige of my faith.' Days passed without word. To her, being an MIA wife was like being in limbo. She found herself only able to pray one thing: 'Help me, dear Father.' She says, 'I hung onto this important truth – that He would help me – and the flickering flame of my candle of faith began to grow.' Then, one day, she noticed a white dove sitting in her yard. It was particularly beautiful, very still and quiet, and a highly uncommon sight in her neighbourhood. She took it as a sign from God that He was, indeed, always near.

For five years, Anne Purcell clung to the fact that God was near. Little did she know that during those years before she was reunited with her husband, he was whispering to her from a POW cell, 'Anne, find solace and strength in the Lord.'

A man is never in worse company than when he flies into a rage and is beside himself.

A quick-tempered man
does foolish things . . .
Proverbs 14:17 (NIV)

A little girl was once in a very bad mood. She took her frustration out on her younger brother, at first just teasing him, but eventually, punching him, pulling his hair, and kicking him in the shins. The boy could take it all – and even dish back a few blows – until the kicking began. That hurt! And he went crying to his mother, complaining about what his sister had done.

The mother came to the little girl and said, 'Mary, why have you let Satan put it into your heart to pull your brother's hair and kick his shins?'

The little girl thought it over for a moment and then answered, 'Well, Mother, maybe Satan did put it into my heart to pull Tommy's hair . . . but kicking his shins was my own idea.'

All the evil in the world doesn't come from direct satanic involvement. Much of it comes from the heart of man. What we do with our anger, feelings of hatred, and frustrations is subject to our *will*. We can choose how we will respond to stress, or to the behaviour of others. Our challenge is to *govern* our emotions; otherwise, they will rule in tyranny over us.

Success in marriage
is more than finding
the right person.
It's becoming
the right person.

But you, man of God, flee from all this,
and pursue righteousness, godliness, faith,
love, endurance and gentleness.
1 Timothy 6:11 (NIV)

In Thornton Wilder's play *The Skin of Our Teeth*, the character Mrs Antrobus says to her husband, 'I didn't marry you because you were perfect . . . I married you because you gave me a promise.'

She then takes off her ring and looks at it, saying, 'That promise made up for your faults and the promise I gave you made up for mine. Two imperfect people got married, and it was the promise that made the marriage.'

In every marriage, no matter how well the two people know one another, great mysteries remain! Very often, each person comes to the marriage:

- not fully knowing himself or herself,
- not fully knowing about life, and
- not fully knowing about his or her spouse.

What is unknown therefore is far greater than what is known!

Becoming a faithful, loving spouse not only takes courage and faith, but patience and a desire to keep learning and growing. Better than the question, 'What kind of spouse do I desire to have?' is the question, 'What kind of spouse do I aspire to be?'

Failure in people is
caused more by lack
of determination than
lack in talent.

And let us not be weary in well doing:
for in due season we shall reap,
if we faint not.
Galatians 6:9 (AV)

In 1982, in America, internal-medicine resident Barry Marshall was frustrated that there was no cure for his patients with ulcers. Then, while studying a stomach biopsy, he saw organisms resembling *Campylobacter* bacteria, first identified by his hospital's pathologist, Dr J. Robin Warren. Warren and Marshall studied 100 ulcer patients for a year, and found the bacteria in 87 per cent of the cases. Leading specialists, however, insisted the bacteria developed *after* the specimens were removed. For decades, clinical researchers had concluded that ulcers were based on weak stomach linings. Marshall's bacterial theory was snubbed.

Warren and Marshall cultured the bacteria for observation and found that a combination of bismuth and antibiotics destroyed it. Again, this report was met with scepticism. Marshall reported study after study. Still, doctors refused to conduct clinical trials. Finally, trials began in 1986, four years after Marshall's initial findings. These studies confirmed both Marshall's bacterial theory and his treatment methods.

Because a young internist 'wouldn't accept no' from the medical community, the vast majority of ulcers, and some stomach cancers, can now be treated successfully.

A man is rich according to
what he is, not according to
what he has.

One man pretends to be rich,
yet has nothing;
another pretends to be poor,
yet has great wealth.
Proverbs 13:7 (NIV)

Fulton Oursler told a story of an old nurse who was born a slave on the eastern shore of Maryland. She had not only attended Fulton's birth, but that of his mother. He credits her for teaching him the greatest lesson he ever learned about giving thanks and finding contentment. Recalls Oursler:

I remember her as she sat at the kitchen table in our house; the hard, old brown hands folded across her starched apron, the glistening eyes, and the husky old whispering voice, saying 'Much obliged, Lord, for my vittles.'
'Anna,' I asked, 'what's a vittle?'
'It's what I've got to eat and drink – that's vittles,' the old nurse replied.
'But you'd get your vittles whether you thanked the Lord or not.'
'Sure,' said Anna, 'but it makes everything taste better to be thankful.'

Poverty is not a state of the wallet for many people, but a state of mind. Do you think of yourself as being rich or poor today? What is it that you truly count as 'wealth' in your life? If you list things that are not material in nature, you are probably very wealthy indeed!

Life can only be understood by looking backward, but it must be lived by looking forward.

But Jesus said to him, No one, having put his hand to the plough, and looking back, is fit for the kingdom of God.
Luke 9:62 (NKJ)

On New Year's Day 1929, Georgia Tech played the University of California in the Rose Bowl. In the first half, Roy Riegels recovered a fumble for California, but he became confused about direction and ran the wrong way. One of his team-mates tackled him just yards before he scored for the opposing team. When California tried to punt, Tech blocked the kick and scored a safety, which became the winning margin.

During half-time, the Cal players sat quietly, waiting to hear what the coach had to say. He was uncharacteristically quiet. Riegels put his blanket around his shoulders, stayed in a corner, put his face in his hands, and cried like a baby. Three minutes before playing time, Coach Price looked at the team and said simply, 'Men, the same team that played the first half will start the second.'

The players filed onto the field, but Riegels did not budge. 'Roy, didn't you hear me?' the coach asked.

Riegels responded, 'I couldn't face that crowd in the stadium to save my life.' Coach Price put his hand on Roy's shoulder and said, 'Roy, get up and go on back; the game is only half over.' Tech men to this day will tell you they have never seen a man play football as Roy Riegels played that second half.

Success comes in cans; failures comes in can'ts.

I can do all things through Christ who strengthens me.
Philippians 4:13 (NKJ)

Perhaps more than any other leader in the twentieth century, Winston Churchill rallied a nation to believe in what it *could* do. His speeches during World War II not only express resolution, but a profound peace of mind and a feeling of 'rightness'. Here are some of his words to England and the world:

> You ask what is our policy? I will say: It is to wage war, by sea, land, and air, with all our might and all the strength that God can give us . . . You ask, What is our aim? I can answer in one word: Victory . . . at all costs, victory in spite of all terror, victory however long and hard the road may be; for without victory there is no survival . . .

> We shall go on to the end, we shall fight in France, we shall fight on the seas and oceans, we shall fight with growing confidence and growing strength in the air, we shall defend our island, whatever the cost may be; we shall fight on the beaches, we shall fight on the landing grounds, we shall fight in the fields and in the streets, we shall fight in the hills; we shall never surrender.

What wonderful words to adapt to any fight against evil!

Sometimes we are so busy
adding up our troubles that
we forget to count our
blessings.

I will remember the deeds of the LORD;
yes, I will remember your miracles
of long ago.
I will meditate on all your works
and consider all your mighty deeds.
Psalm 77: 11,12 (NIV)

For decades, Grandpa had been stubborn and crabby. His wife, children and grandchildren seemed to be able to do nothing that pleased him. As far as he was concerned, life was filled with nothing but bad times and big troubles. Eventually, his family expected only a gruff growl from Grandpa.

Then overnight, Grandpa changed. Gentleness and optimism marked his new personality. Positive words and compliments poured from his lips. He could even be heard giving joyful praise to the Lord. One of the family members noted, 'I think maybe Grandpa found religion.' Another replied, 'Maybe so, but maybe it's something else. I'm going to ask him what has happened.' The young man went to his grandfather and said 'Gramps, what has caused you to change so suddenly?'

'Well, son,' the old man replied, 'I've been striving in the face of incredible problems all my life – and for what? The hope of a contented mind. It's done no good, nope, not one bit, so . . . I've decided to be contented without it.'

Never start counting your troubles until you've counted at least a hundred of your blessings. By that time, you probably won't think you have troubles!

Falling down doesn't make you a failure, but staying down does.

For though a righteous man falls seven times, he rises again . . .
Proverbs 24:16 (NIV)

Most people know that Thomas Edison conducted countless experiments with countless kinds of materials in search of an effective filament to use in carbon incandescent lamps. As each fibre failed, he would toss it out of the window. Ultimately, the pile of failures reached to the second storey of his house.

One day in 1879, some thirteen months after his first failure, he succeeded in finding a filament that would stand the stress of electric current. Here's how: Edison casually picked up a bit of lampblack, mixed it with tar, rolled it into a thin thread, and thought, *Why not try a carbonised cotton fibre?* He worked for five hours to make a fibre but it broke in two before he removed the mould. He used two spools of cotton thread before a perfect strand emerged, only to be ruined when he tried to place it in a glass tube. He continued without sleep for two days and nights before he managed to slip one of the carbonised threads into a vacuum-sealed bulb. Turning on the current, he saw the glow of electric light that we now take for granted.

A failure doesn't need to mark the end. It can be one step closer to the success you desire!

If a task is once begun,
never leave it 'till it's done.
Be the labour great or small,
do it well or not at all.

I have glorified You on the earth. I have
finished the work which You
have given Me to do.
John 17:4 (NKJ)

The order from the head teacher was abrupt: 'The classroom needs sweeping. Take the broom and sweep it.'

Young Booker T. Washington knew that this was his chance. He swept the room three times, and then dusted the furniture four times. When the head teacher came back to evaluate his work, she inspected the floor closely and then used her handkerchief to rub the woodwork around the walls, the table and the students' benches. When she could not find one speck of dust anywhere in the room, she said quietly, 'I guess you will do to enter this institution.'

Cleaning a classroom was nothing less than Booker T. Washington's entrance examination to Hampton Institute in Virginia. In later years, he would recall this as the turning point in his life. He wrote in his autobiography, *Up From Slavery*, 'I have passed several examinations since then, but I have always felt that this was the best one I ever passed.'

Slacking off, goofing off, and dozing off rarely open doors of opportunity. Those doors are opened best by a consistently excellent effort. Give the world an effort of that calibre today!

Time is more valuable than money because time is irreplaceable.

Making the most of the time,
because the days are evil.
Ephesians 5:16 (RSV)

How many times have we said, or heard others say, 'Manāna. I'll do it tomorrow.' Sometimes people put off doing today what they know or want to do because they don't think they know enough or can perform well enough. The fact is, there is no 'magic age' at which excellence emerges or quality surfaces.

Thomas Jefferson was 33 when he drafted the Declaration of Independence. Benjamin Franklin was 26 when he wrote *Poor Richard's Almanac*. Charles Dickens was 24 when he began his *Pickwick Papers* and 25 when he wrote *Oliver Twist*. Isaac Newton was 24 when he formulated the law of gravitation.

A second danger is to think that creativity and invention belong to the young. This is equally untrue! Emmanuel Kant wrote his finest philosophical works at age 74. Verdi at 80 produced *Falstaff* and at 85, *Ave Maria*. Goethe was 80 when he completed *Faust*. Tennyson was 80 when he wrote *Crossing the Bar* and Michelangelo completed his greatest work at 87. At 90, Justice Holmes was still writing brilliant Supreme Court opinions.

Seize the day! Redeem the 'now' moments of your life. The moment you wait for may never arrive. The moment once past will never return.

The best way to forget your own problems is to help someone solve his.

None of you should think only of his own affairs, but consider other people's interests also.
Philippians 2:4 (JBP)

Sadhu Sundar Singh and a companion were travelling through a pass high in the Himalayan Mountains when they came across a body lying in the snow. They checked for vital signs and discovered the man still alive, but barely so. Sundar Singh prepared to stop and help this unfortunate traveller, but his companion objected, saying, 'We shall lose our lives if we burden ourselves with him.' Sundar Singh, however, could not think of leaving the man to die in the snow without an attempted rescue on his part. His companion quickly bade him farewell and walked on.

Sundar Singh lifted the poor traveller onto his back. With great exertion on his part – made even greater by the high altitude and snowy conditions – he carried the man onward. As he walked, the heat cast off by his body began to warm the frozen man. He revived and soon both were walking together side by side, each holding the other up, and in turn, each giving body heat to the other. Before long they came upon yet another traveller's body lying in the snow. Upon closer inspection, they discovered him to be dead, frozen by the cold.

He was Sundar Singh's original travelling companion.

Don't forget, by reaching out to help others you usually forget your own problems.

God can heal a broken
heart, but he has to have all
the pieces.

My son, give me your heart . . .
Proverbs 23:26 (RSV)

A boy once said to God, 'I've been thinking, and I know what I want when I become a man.' He proceeded to give God his list: to live in a big house with two Saint Bernards and a garden . . . marry a blue-eyed, tall, beautiful woman . . . have three sons – one who would be a senator, one a scientist and one an Olympic gold medalist. He also wanted to be an adventurer who climbed tall mountains . . . and to drive a red Ferrari.

As it turned out, the boy hurt his knee one day while playing football. He no longer could climb trees, much less mountains. He married a beautiful and kind woman, who was short with brown eyes. Because of his business, he lived in a city apartment, took taxis and travelled on the underground. He had three loving daughters, and they adopted a fluffy cat. One daughter became a nurse, another an artist, and the third a music teacher.

One morning the man awoke and remembered his boyhood dream. He became extremely depressed, so depressed that he became very ill. Close to death from a broken heart, he called out to God, 'Remember when I was a boy and told you all the things I wanted? Why didn't you give me those things?'

'I could have.' said God, 'but I wanted to make you happy.'

Remember, God wants the best for us. Trust him with your whole heart – he's the original heart surgeon.

Authority makes some people grow – and others just swell.

But he that is greatest among you shall be your servant. And whosoever shall exalt himself shall be abased; and he that shall humble himself shall be exalted.

Matthew 23: 11,12 (AV)

Everybody knows of Isaac Newton's famed encounter with a falling apple, and how Newton introduced the laws of gravity and revolutionized astronomical studies. But few know that if it weren't for Edmund Halley, the world may never have heard of Newton. Halley was the one who challenged Newton to think through his original theories. He corrected Newton's mathematical errors and prepared geometrical figures to support his discoveries. It was Halley who coaxed the hesitant Newton to write his great work, *Mathematical Principles of Natural Philosophy*. And it was Halley who edited and supervised its publication, financing its printing even though Newton was wealthier.

Historians have called Halley's relationship with Newton one of the most selfless examples in science. Newton began almost immediately to reap the rewards of prominence; Halley received little credit. He did use the principles Newton developed to predict the orbit and return of a comet that would later bear his name, but since Halley's Comet only returns every 76 years, few hear his name. Still, Halley didn't care who received credit as long as the cause of science was advanced. He was content to live without fame.

Sometimes just the reward of *what* we are doing far outweighs the recognitgion we often think we need to have.

Be more concerned with
what God thinks about you
than what people think
about you.

*Then Peter and the other apostles
answered and said, 'We ought
to obey God rather than men.'*
Acts 5:29 (AV)

Jenny Lind was known as 'The Swedish Nightingale' during her very successful career as an operatic singer. She became one of the wealthiest artists of her time, yet she left the stage at a time when she was singing her best. And she never returned to it.

Countless people speculated as to the reason for her leaving, and most people wondered how she could give up so much applause, fame and money. For her part, she seemed content to live in privacy in a home by the sea.

One day a friend found her on the beach, her Bible on her knees, looking out into the glorious glow of a sunset. As they talked, the friend asked, 'Madam Goldschmidt, how is that you ever came to abandon the stage at the height of your success?'

She answered quietly, 'When every day it made me think less of this (laying a finger on her Bible) and nothing at all of that (pointing to the sunset), what else could I do?'

The world may never understand your decision to follow God's way. But then, perhaps God cannot understand a decision to pursue what the world offers.

The trouble with the guy who talks too fast is that he often says something he hasn't thought of yet.

Do not be quick with your mouth,
do not be hasty in your heart
to utter anything before God.
God is in heaven
and you are on earth,
so let your words be few.
Ecclesiastes 5:2 (NIV)

Tom Kelly managed the Minnesota Twins to a World Series title in 1987, his first full season as their manager – and then managed them to their second world championship in 1991. Yet to watch him at work, critics have wondered if his vital signs have been stolen. Asked one sports writer, 'How has T.K. *managed* all this, while lowering his blood pressure to the equivalent of the water pressure in your first apartment? He doesn't chew on fingernails or Rolaids or tobacco or his players. How?'

One of Kelly's trademarks is that he is a man of few words. He enjoys throwing and batting practice every day, in part because he believes that every minute he is throwing, he doesn't have to speak to the media. 'I'm not really intelligent.' T.K. claims. 'I have a year and a half college. But I have enough common sense to realise that I'm not intelligent. I realise that if I keep talking, I'll eventually say something dumb. So I don't give myself a lot of opportunities to open my mouth and stick my foot in it.'

Tom Kelly is far from dumb. So is any person who is smart enough to limit what he says.

The best way to get the last word is to apologise.

If you have been trapped by what you said,
ensnared by the words of your mouth,
then do this, my son, to free yourself,
since you have fallen into your
neighbour's hands:
Go and humble yourself;
press your plea with your neighbour!
Proverbs 6:2,3 (NIV)

A woman in a smart car waited patiently in a crowded carpark for a parking space. She drove up and down between rows until finally she saw a man with a load of packages head for his car. She followed him and parked behind him, waiting while he opened his boot and loaded it. Finally he got into his car and backed out. Just as she was preparing to pull forward into the space, a young man in a little sports car – coming from the opposite direction – turned in front of her, zipped into the space, got out of his car, and started walking away.

The woman was livid. She shouted from her big luxury car, 'Hey, young man! I was waiting for that parking place.'

The teenager responded, 'Sorry lady, but that's how it is when you're young and quick.' She instantly put her car in gear, slammed her foot on the accelerator and crashed into the sports car, crushing its right rear bumper. Now it was the young man's turn to jump up and down, shouting, 'What are you doing?' The woman in the smart car calmly responded, 'Well, son, that's how it is when you're old and rich.'

Most of the world's problems and conflicts could probably be resolved if, instead of retaliation and revenge, apologies were made all around.

The train of failure usually runs on the track of laziness.

If a man is lazy, the rafters sag;
if his hands are idle, the house leaks.
Ecclesiastes 10:18 (NIV)

Success in business is often closely associated with a person's courage and ability to recover from his or her most recent failure!

In 1928 a 33-year-old man by the name of Paul Galvin found himself staring at failure ... again. He had failed in business twice at this point, his competitors having forced him to fold his latest venture in the storage-battery business. Convinced however that he still had a marketable idea, Galvin attended the auction of his own business. With $750 he had managed to raise, he bought back the battery eliminator portion of the inventory. With it he built a new company ... one in which he succeeded ... one from which he eventually retired ... one that became a household word: Motorola. Upon his retirement, Galvin advised others: 'Do not fear mistakes. You will know failure – continue to reach out.'

A failure isn't truly a failure until you stop trying. If a venture begins to slow down, try speeding up your efforts. Consider the child who allows a bicycle to slow to a halt. Eventually the bicycle wobbles to the point where the child falls off. The key to turning around the crash? Faster peddling! The same holds true for many an enterprise.

When confronted with a Goliath-sized problem, which way do you respond: 'He's too big to hit', or like David, 'He's too big to miss'?

. . . The LORD that delivered me out of the paw of the lion, and out of the paw of the bear, he will deliver me out of the hand of this Philistine.

1 Samuel 17:37 (AV)

One day the Pahouins brought a giant native in chains to Albert Schweitzer's hospital. In a fit of madness, N'Tschambi had killed a woman. Reaching down to help the man to the landing from the boat, Schweitzer saw fear and sadness in his face. When others refused his order to remove the man's chains, he did it himself. He then prescribed sedatives to N'Tschambi, and the fearful man gratefully accepted them. That night he slept for the first time without nightmares.

N'Tschambi became a model patient and soon Schweitzer gave him periods of freedom outside his room, to which he often returned voluntarily if he became agitated. Still, any task he was given, he tackled with a fierce energy that frightened the staff. One day Schweitzer gave him an axe and asked him to help him make a clearing. N'Tschambi drew back in alarm, stating he was afraid to touch the axe for fear of what he might do with it. Schweitzer replied, 'If I'm not afraid, why should you be?' The two then went into the jungle as the entire hospital watched. Hours later, they returned, N'Tschambi's big body dripping with sweat but with a radiant smile on his lips. The giant inside him had been felled by kindness and the faith another human being had put in him!

Forget yourself for others and others will not forget you!

So in everything, do to others what you would have them do to you, for this sums up the Law and the Prophets.
Matthew 7:12 (NIV)

Reporters and city officials gathered at a Chicago railway station one afternoon in 1953. The person they were meeting was the 1952 Nobel Peace Prize winner. A few minutes after the train came to a stop, a giant of a man – six foot four – with bushy hair and a large moustache stepped from the train. Cameras flashed. City officials approached him with hands outstretched. Various ones began telling him how honoured they were to meet him.

The man politely thanked them and then, looking over their heads, he asked if he could be excused for a moment. He quickly walked through the crowd until he reached the side of an elderly black woman who was struggling with two large suitcases. He picked up the bags and with a smile, escorted the woman to a bus. After helping her aboard, he wished her a safe journey. Returning to the greeting party he apologised, 'Sorry to have kept you waiting.'

The man was Dr Albert Schweitzer, the famous missionary doctor who had spent his life helping the poor in Africa. In response to Schweitzer's action, one member of the reception committee said with great admiration to the reporter standing next to him. 'That's the first time I ever saw a sermon walking.'

The secret of success is to start from scratch and keep on scratching.

And the seed in the good soil, these are the ones who have heard the word in an honest and good heart, and hold it fast, and bear fruit with perseverance.
Luke 8:15 (NASB)

Hard work means nothing to a hen. Regardless of what business prognosticators say about the price of eggs . . . regardless of what others expect of her . . . regardless of fluctuations in the commodities market . . . she keeps on digging and laying eggs.

If the ground is hard, she scratches harder.
If it's dry, she digs deeper.
If it's wet, she digs where it is dry.
If she strikes a rock, she digs around it.
If she gets a few more hours of daylight in the farmyard, she digs a few more hours.
Have you ever seen a pessimistic hen?
Have you ever seen a hen cackle in disgust at the prospect of her job?
Did you ever hear one cluck because the work was hard, the conditions were poor, and some of her eggs were taken from her before they hatched?

No.
Hens save their breath for digging. They save their cackles for the eggs that are laid.

The secret of contentment is the realisation that life is a gift not a right.

But godliness with contentment is great gain. For we brought nothing into this world, and it is certain we can carry nothing out.
1 Timothy 6:6,7 (AV)

At age 14, Andrea Jaeger won her first professional tennis tournament. At 18, she reached the finals of Wimbledon. At 19, a bad shoulder all but ended her career. Many a world-class athlete might have become bitter or discontented with life at that point. Jaeger, however, turned her competitive spirit to a new endeavour, a non-profit-making organisation called Kids' Stuff Foundation that attempts to bring joy to children suffering from cancer and other life-threatening illnesses. Her work there has also inspired her to take correspondence courses in nursing and child psychology.

Jaeger not only created the programme, but runs it full-time, year-round, unpaid. 'I'm inspired by these brave kids, and humbled,' she has said. 'They lose their health, their friends and sometimes their lives. And yet their spirit never wavers. They look at life as a gift. The rest of us sometimes look at ourselves as a gift to life.'

'You get very spoiled on the tour,' she adds with a twinkle in her eye. 'The courtesy cars, the five-star hotels, the thousands of people clapping you when you hit a good shot. It's easy to forget what's important in life . . . I forget it a lot less lately.'

No one ever said on their deathbed: I wish I had spent more time at work!

I hated all the things I had toiled for under the sun, because I must leave them to the one who comes after me.
Ecclesiastes 2:18 (NIV)

Whatever you do, work at it with all your heart, as working for the Lord, not for men.
Colossians 3:23 (NIV)

Dutch author and priest, Henri Nouwen, admits in his book *In the Name of Jesus* that he felt as if he was in a 'rut' in his life for more than 20 years. Nouwen seemed to have it made, with an outstanding academic career and a noble field of study. Yet, he said,

> As I entered into my fifties . . . I came face to face with a simple question, Did becoming older bring me closer to Jesus? After 25 years of priesthood, I found myself praying poorly, living somewhat isolated from other people, and very much preoccupied with burning issues . . . I woke up one day with the realisation that I was living in a very dark place.

Nouwen asked God to show him where He wanted him to go and the Lord make it clear to him that he should leave his prestigious role as a distinguished professor and join the L'Arche communities for mentally handicapped people. In Nouwen's words, 'God said, "Go and live among the poor in spirit, and they will heal you."' So he did. He faced numerous lessons, some painful, a few humiliating, but in all, he learned how to be a humble servant and a compassionate, caring friend. Nouwen came to realise: it's not work that makes a person, but rather, relationships.

True faith and courage are like a kite – an opposing wind raises it higher.

But they that wait upon the LORD shall renew their strength; they shall mount up with wings as eagles; they shall run, and not be weary; and they shall walk, and not faint.
Isaiah 40:31 (AV)

Norma Zimmer, the well-known singer for Lawrence Welk, had a difficult childhood as a result of her parents' drinking. Singing was her escape! As a high school senior, Norma was invited to be a featured soloist at the University Christian Church in Seattle. When her parents heard she was going to sing a particular song, they both insisted on attending the service. She tells about that morning, 'I stole glances at the congregation, trying to find my parents . . . then in horror I saw them – weaving down the aisle in a state of dishevelled intoxication. They were late. Few empty seats were left . . . The congregation stared. I don't know how I ever got through that morning.'

After she sang and took her seat, her heart pounding and her cheeks burning from embarrassment, the pastor preached: 'God is our refuge and strength, a tested help in time of trouble.' She says, 'My own trouble seemed to bear down on me with tremendous weight . . . I realised how desperate life in our family was without God, and that day I recommitted my life to Him . . . Jesus came into my life not only as Saviour but for daily strength and direction.'

Don't let a difficult time box you in. Let it drive you to Jesus.

In order to receive the direction from God you must be able to receive the correction from God.

. . . My son, do not make light of the Lord's discipline, and do not lose heart when he rebukes you, because the Lord disciplines those he loves, and he punishes everyone he accepts as a son . . .
Hebrews 12:5-6 (NIV)

As a professional stock-car racer, Darrell Waltrip was once proud of his image as 'the guy folks loved to hate'. When crowds booed, he'd just kick the dirt and smile. Then things began to change. He miraculously survived a Daytona 500 crash. He began going to church with his wife, Stevie. He and Stevie began to try to have a family. Stevie, however, suffered four miscarriages.

One day their pastor came to visit. He asked, 'Your car is sponsored by a beer company. Is that the image you want?' Darrell had never thought about it. He had always loved watching kids admire his car, but as he thought about it he discovered that he *did* care about his image. He thought, *If Stevie's and my prayers were answered for a child, what kind of dad would I be?* He remembered his pastor's admonition to 'walk the walk, not just talk the talk'.

He didn't know what to do to convince the car owner to change sponsors, but amazingly, an opportunity opened for him to sign with a new racing team sponsored by a detergent company! After much thought and more prayer, he switched teams. Two years later, daughter Jessica was born, and a few years later, daughter Sarah. In 1989 he won Daytona.

Those who bring sunshine
to the lives of others cannot
keep it from themselves.

Do not deceive yourselves; no one makes a
fool of God. People will reap exactly what
they sow.
Galations 6:7 (GNB)

The story is told of a man and woman who gave a sizeable contribution to the church to honour the memory of their son who lost his life in the war. When the announcement was made to the congregation of the generous donation, a woman whispered to her husband, 'Let's give the same amount in honour of each of our boys.'

The husband replied, 'What are you talking about? Neither of our sons was killed in the war.'

'Exactly,' said the woman. 'Let's give it as an expression of our gratitude to God for sparing their lives!'

What we give to charitable concerns during our life produces benefit in three directions: (1) it helps those in need, (2) it inspires others to give, and, (3) it forms an inner character in the giver – one marked by less selfishness and fewer materialistic tendencies, greater generosity and a heightened awareness of and concern for other people.

Keep in mind that when you give, you are ultimately giving to *people*, even though your gift might be made to an institution or organization. churches and other charities are made up of people. Your giving brings sunshine to the lives of others and will return to you.

No man ever really finds out what he believes in until he begins to instruct his children.

Fathers, do not exasperate your children; instead, bring them up in the training and instruction of the Lord.
Ephesians 6:4 (NIV)

A dog once wandered to a preacher's home, and his three sons played with it, fed it and soon became quite fond of it. It so happened that the dog had three white hairs on its tail. One day, the preacher and his sons spotted an advertisement in the local newspaper about a lost dog. The description of the stray they had taken in matched perfectly.

The minister said, 'In the presence of my three boys, we carefully separated the three white hairs and removed them from the dog's tail.'

The real owner of the dog eventually discovered where his stray pooch had gone and he came to claim him. The dog showed every sign of recognising his owner, so the man was ready to take him away. At that point, the minister spoke up and asked, 'Didn't you say the dog would be known by three white hairs in its tail?' The owner, unable to find the identifying feature, was forced to admit that this dog didn't fully fit the description of his lost dog and left.

Years passed and the minister noted with sadness, 'We kept the dog, but I lost my three boys for Christ that day.' His sons no longer had confidence in what their father professed to be true.

Remember, your children watch the choices you make in all areas of your life and base their opinion of you on them. Be a person of integrity – one they will admire.

Don't mistake activity for achievement. Busyness does not equal productiveness.

But Martha was distracted by all the preparations that had to be made. She came to him and asked, 'Lord, don't you care that my sister has left me to do the work by myself? Tell her to help me!' 'Martha, Martha,' the Lord answered, 'you are worried and upset about many things, but only one thing is needed. Mary has chosen what is better, and it will not be taken away from her.'
Luke 10:40–42 (NIV)

In April 1973, the Park Centre YMCA in Midland, Texas, asked for volunteers to help repair seventeen run-down homes in the city. The effort was so successful that Midlanders made it an annual event. After volunteers had completed repairs on one home, the owner opened her front door and exclaimed, 'It's just like Christmas in April.' The name stuck.

'Christmas in April' has not only made hundreds of homes more liveable in this West Texas oil town, but it helped bring the city together. Men and women, young and old, black, Hispanic and white volunteers build community spirit as they scrape, caulk, plaster, paint, hammer and roof together. Said one volunteer, 'It's a blessing to us as well as to those we help. There's no better way to get to know someone than to sit up on a roof with him all day.' One year 398 gallons of paint, 600 pounds of nails, 224 squares of roofing materials, 60 doors, and $10,000 of lumber were used to repair 84 homes.

Midlanders have learned how to be *both* busy and productive by pulling together to help others. In most instances of our lives, work need not be left undone or goals sacrificed. Priorities simply need to be realigned.

It's the little things in life that determine the big things.

. . . You've been trustworthy over a few things, now I'm going to put you in charge of many more. Come in and share your master's rejoicing.
Matthew 25:21 (JBP)

Several centuries ago, the Emperor of Japan commissioned a Japanese artist to paint a particular species of bird for him. Months passed, then years. Finally, the Emperor went personally to the artist's studio to ask for an explanation.

The artist set a blank canvas on the easel and within fifteen minutes, had completed a painting of a bird. It was a masterpiece! The Emperor, admiring both the painting and the artist's great skill, asked why there had been such a long delay.

The artist then went from cabinet to cabinet in his studio. He pulled from them armloads of drawings of feathers, tendons, wings, feet, claws, eyes, beaks – virtually every aspect of a bird, from virtually every angle. He placed these silently before the Emperor, who nodded an understanding. The magnificence of any 'whole' can never be greater than the magnificence of any singular detail.

To have an excellent life, strive for an excellent year. Within that year, strive for an excellent month, and within that month, strive for an excellent day. Within the day, strive for an excellent hour. An excellent life is the sum of many excellent moments!

The doors of opportunity
are marked 'Push' and
'Pull'.

*The sluggard craves and gets nothing, but
the desires of the diligent are fully
satisfied.*
Proverbs 13:4 (NIV)

A man once went with a friend for a ride out in the country. They drove off the main road and through a grove of orange trees to a mostly uninhabited piece of land. A few horses grazed there amidst a couple of old shacks. Walter stopped the car and began to describe vividly the things he was going to build on the land. He wanted his friend Arthur to buy some of the land surrounding his project. Walter explained to his friend, 'I can handle the main project myself. It will take all my money, but . . . I want you to have the first chance at this surrounding acreage, because in the next five years it will increase in value several hundred times.'

Arthur thought to himself, *Who in the world is going to drive twenty-five miles for this crazy project? His dream has taken the best of his common sense.* He mumbled something about a tight-money situation and promised to look into the deal later. 'Later on will be too late,' Walter cautioned. 'You'd better move on it right now.' Arthur failed, however, to act.

And so it was that Art Linkletter turned down the opportunity to buy the land that surrounded what became Disneyland, the land his friend Walt Disney had tried to talk him into.

Most opportunities take a step of faith whether for financial or relationship investments.

You cannot win if you do not begin.

Now finish the work, so that your eager willingness to do it may be matched by your completion of it, according to your means.
2 Corinthians 8:11 (NIV)

Novelist A. J. Cronin had been in practice as a physician for almost ten years when he developed a gastric ulcer that required complete rest. He went to a farm in the Scottish Highlands to recuperate. He says, 'The first few days of leisure were pleasant enough, but soon the enforced idleness of Fyne Farm became insufferable . . . I had often, at the back of my mind, nursed the vague illusion that I might write. I had actually thought out the theme of a novel – the tragic record of man's egotism and bitter pride . . .

'Upstairs in my cold, clean bedroom was a scrubbed deal table and a very hard chair. Next morning I found myself in this chair, facing a new exercise book open upon the table, slowly becoming aware that, short of dog-Latin prescriptions, I had never composed a significant phrase in all my life. It was a discouraging thought as I picked up my pen. Never mind, I began.'

Even though Cronin struggled to write 500 words a day and eventually threw his first draft on the farm's rubbish heap, he finished *Hatter's Castle*. The book was dramatised, translated into 22 languages, and sold some five million copies. The world had lost a physician, but gained a novelist.

The best way to be successful is to follow the advice you give others.

He who ignores discipline despises himself, but whoever heeds correction gains understanding.
Proverbs 15:32 (NIV)

An officer in the navy had dreamed from child-hood of commanding a great battleship one day. He finally achieved his dream and was given commission of the newest and proudest ship in the fleet.

One stormy night, the captain was on duty on the bridge when he spotted a strange light rapidly closing with his own vessel. As his ship ploughed through the giant waves, the light rose and fell just above the horizon of the sea. He ordered his signalman to flash a message to the unidentified craft on his port side, 'Alter your course ten degrees to the south.'

Within seconds a reply came, 'Alter your course ten degrees to the north.' Determined that his ship would never take a backseat to any other, the captain snapped a second order, 'Alter course ten degrees – I am the CAPTAIN!' The response was beamed back, 'Alter your course ten degrees – I am Seaman Third Class Smith.' By this time the light was growing ever brighter and larger.

Infuriated, the captain grabbed the signal light and personally signalled, 'Alter course. I am a battleship.' The reply came just as quickly, 'Alter your course. I am a lighthouse.'

Contentment isn't getting
what we want but being
satisfied with what we have.

Not that I speak in regard to need,
for I have learned in whatever state I am,
to be content.
Philippians 4:11 (NKJ)

The story is told of a farmer who had lived on the same farm all his life. It was a good farm with fertile soil, but with the passing of years, the farmer began to think, *Maybe there's something better for me.* He set out to find an even better plot of land to farm.

Every day he found a new reason for criticising some feature of his old farm. Finally, he decided to sell. He listed the farm with an estate agent who promptly prepared an advertisement emphasising all the many advantages of the acreage: ideal location, modern equipment, healthy stock, acres of fertile ground, high yields on crops, well-kept barns and pens, nice two-storey house on a hill above the pasture.

When the estate agent called to read the ad to the farmer for his approval prior to placing it in the local paper, the farmer heard him out. When he had finished, he cried, 'Hold everything! I've changed my mind. I'm not going to sell. Why, I've been looking for a place just like that all my life!'

When you start identifying the good traits of any person, situation or organisation, you are likely to find that they far outweigh the bad. Focus on what you have, What you have *not* will likely seem insignificant.

Too many people quit looking for work when they find a job.

One who is slack in his work
is brother to one who destroys.
Proverbs 18:9 (NIV)

In her autobiography, *Who Could Ask For Anything More*, Ethel Merman tells how Cole Porter and a buddy of his had a game they played with Irving Berlin. Says Merman, 'When they see Irving coming they look at their wrist watches and make a five-dollar bet. Then they pick a topic and start in on it. Anything will do: Victor Moore, Mount Everest, volcanoes, Eskimo Pies, Philadelphia, the Dalai Lama of Tibet. The bet is based on the number of minutes it will take Irving to bring the conversation around to one of his own songs, no matter where it starts. The average time is said to be less than five minutes.'

Merman notes, 'I wouldn't go so far as to call this ego on Irving's part. It's just that he's so absorbed in his work and so intense about it that what he writes is the most important thing in the world to him . . . To me, he doesn't seem so much egotistical as enthusiastic.'

Interesting that Cole Porter would play such a trick since he once told an interviewer, 'If I don't seem to be listening to what you're saying, it's because I'm writing a song in the back of my head . . . Some people think work is a four-letter word. I don't.'

You can't take your money with you, but you can send it on ahead.

Do not lay up for yourselves treasures on earth, where moth and rust destroy and where thieves break in and steal; but lay up for yourselves treasures in heaven, where neither moth nor rust destroys and where thieves do not break in and steal.
Matthew 6:19,20 (NKJ)

In the mid-nineteenth century, in the USA, tea cost about a dollar a pound, making it an expensive staple. George Hartford and George Gilman came up with a simple but revolutionary plan to lower the price. They bought tea directly from the ships in New York Harbour. Then, taking a low-percentage profit, they tried to achieve high-volume sales. Their tactics worked. They soon turned their mail-order business into a chain of stores called the Great Atlantic and Pacific Tea Co – A&P.

From the outset, and even with a family of five children, Hartford generously gave thousands of dollars a year to charitable causes, ranging from the Pius X Mission in Skagway, Alaska, to the First Methodist Church in Urbana, Illinois. As his fortune increased, he established a foundation as a conduit for his giving. Hartford's desire was that his contributions should benefit people such as those whose purchases at A&P stores had built his fortunes. Later, he reorganised the foundation to receive his estate, so that by the time he died, bequests to individuals totalled $500,000, with $55 million going to the foundation, including $40 million in A&P stock. Thus, a portion of every dollar spent at an A&P store would eventually be 'donated'. Hartford in many ways is *still* giving his fortune away!

Ability will enable a man to go to the top, but it takes character to keep him there.

The righteousness of the blameless
makes a straight way for them,
but the wicked are brought down
by their own wickedness.
Proverbs 11:5 (NIV)

Convicted Watergate conspirator John Ehrlichman wrote of his experience: 'When I went to jail, nearly two years after the cover-up trial, I had a big self-esteem problem. I was a felon, shorn and scorned, clumping around in a ragged old army uniform, doing pick and shovel work out in the desert. I wondered if anyone thought I was worth any thing . . . For years I had been able to sweep most of my shortcomings and failures under the rug and not face them, but during the two long criminal trials, I spent my days listening to prosecutors tell juries what a bad fellow I was . . . I'd go back to a hotel room and sit alone thinking about what was happening to me. During that time I began to take stock . . . I was wiped out. I had nothing left that had been of value to me – honour, credibility, virtue, recognition, profession.'

Then he began to see himself . . . and to care deeply about his own integrity, his capacity to love and be loved, and his essential worth. He concluded about the Nixon years, 'In a paradoxical way, I'm grateful for them. Somehow I had to see all of that and grow to understand it in order to arrive.' Sadly, the inner character Ehrlichman developed came too late to impact his political career at the top.

Keep a daily check on your character. Of all the abilities you may possess, the one to develop a good character is your greatest.

Your words are windows to your heart.

. . . For a man's words flow out of what fills his heart.
Matthew 12:34 (JBP)

Author J. Allan Petersen tells about a flight he took on a 747 out of Brazil. He was awakened from sleep by a strong voice announcing, 'We have a very serious emergency.' Three engines had stopped because of fuel contamination and the fourth was expected to go at any second. The plane began to drop and turn in the night, preparing for an emergency landing.

At first the situation seemed unreal to Petersen, but when the steward barked, 'Prepare for impact,' he found himself – and everyone around him – praying. As he buried his head in his lap and pulled up his knees, he said, 'Oh God, thank You. Thank You for the incredible privilege of knowing You. Life has been wonderful.' As the plane approached the ground, his last cry was, 'Oh, God, my wife! My children!'

Petersen survived. As he wandered around the air-port in a daze, aching all over, he found he couldn't speak, but his mind was racing. *What were my last words? What was the bottom line?* As he remembered, he had his answer: relationship. Reunited with his wife and sons, he found that all he could say to them over and over was, 'I appreciate you, I appreciate you!'

Listen to what you are saying. Have you told that person who matters most to you how you *really* feel?

A shut mouth gathers no foot.

He who guards his lips guards his life,
but he who speaks rashly will
come to ruin.
Proverbs 13:3 (NIV)

Constance Cameron tells a lesson her mother taught her. One day, when she was about eight, she was playing beside an open window. Inside, Mrs Brown was confiding a personal problem to Constance's mother. After Mrs Brown had gone, the mother realised that Constance had heard everything that had been said. She called her in and said, 'If Mrs Brown had left her purse here today, would we give it to anyone else?'

'Of course not,' the girl said. Her mother went on, 'Mrs Brown left something more precious than her purse today. She left a story that could make many people unhappy. That story is not ours to give to anyone, it is still hers, even though she left it here. So we shall not give it to anyone. Do you understand?'

She did. And from that day on, whenever a friend would share a confidence or even engage in careless gossip, she considered what they said to be the personal property of the other person – and not hers to give to anyone else.

The old saying bears great truth: 'If you don't have something positive to say about someone or something, don't say anything.'

The only fool bigger than
the person who knows it all
is the person who argues
with him.

Whoever corrects a mocker invites insult;
whoever rebukes a wicked man incurs
abuse.
Proverbs 9:7 (NIV)

When Charles Spurgeon was still a young preacher, he was warned about a certain woman with a reputation for being extremely quarrelsome. He was told that she intended to give him a tongue-lashing the moment she saw him next.

Spurgeon said, 'All right, but that's a game two can play.'

Shortly thereafter she met him and began to assault him with a flood of verbal abuse. He simply smiled back at her and said, 'Oh yes, thank you. I am quite well. Thank you for asking. I hope you are the same.'

His remarks were followed by another tirade of know-it-all comments, this time voiced at a slightly higher volume. He responded again, smiling quietly, 'Yes, it does look rather as if it might rain. I think I had better be getting on.'

'Bless the man!' the woman exclaimed and then concluded, 'He's as deaf as a post. What's the use of storming at him!'

Never again did she assault Spurgeon with her arguments. And never did he tell her what he had done! There's no point in arguing with know-it-all people. Better to let them have their say and walk on.

A drowning man does not complain about the size of a lifebelt.

Do all things without murmurings and disputings.
Philippians 2:14 (AV)

On his way home to surprise his mother for All Souls' Day, Mishi Dobos stopped by the family's summer cottage to see what repairs he might undertake next. His eyes fell on the garden well, a solid brick structure four feet in diameter. As he leaned over to peer into the 70-foot shaft with a flashlight, he failed to notice the frosty moss on the well's rim. Within seconds, he had plummeted feet first into the shaft, landing ankle-deep in soft mud.

For three days Mishi shouted for help. Then, on the fourth day, while attempting to make a place to sit, he ripped a carpenter's clamp – a foot-long piece of metal with upturned ends – away from the rotting wood. Mishi thought, *What can I do with this?* Studying the walls, he saw a brick missing on one side. An idea dawned – use the clamp to chip out bricks in a staggered upward fashion and climb out!

Mishi went to work. At best, he could remove three bricks an hour. But brick by brick and a bad fall later – in all, six days and 23 hours after plunging into the well – Mishi swung his leg over the edge of the upper rim, the rusty carpenter's clamp in his hand.

Look around. What normally useless object might God lead you to use with cleverness and strength?

Blessed is he who, having nothing to say, refrains from giving wordy evidence of the fact.

*The tongue of the wise
uses knowledge rightly,
But the mouth of fools
pours forth foolishness.*
Proverbs 15:2 (NKJ)

In the eighteenth century, Dr Johann Beringer was a professor of natural philosophy at the University of Warzburg, Germany. He concluded that fossils were not linked to previously living animals, as some were advocating, but rather, that they were unique 'creations', each part of a divine message planted into the earth by the Lord at the time of Creation. He advocated that man study the fossils with the intent of uncovering the meaning of God's buried message.

His students decided to make and then implant into a nearby hillside, hundreds of grotesque clay forms, some of which were fossil-like, others of which had writing on them. One of the clay figures was actually signed by 'Jehovah'.

The doctor was so convinced that his 'find' had divine meaning that he published a book on the subject, ignoring the repeated confessions of his students as to their prank. He chided his students for attempting to undermine his work and rob him of the fame due him. It was not until Beringer discovered a 'fossil' bearing his own name that he accepted the hoax for what it had been. And for the rest of his life, he spent a small fortune trying to buy back the existing copies of his own book.

Luck: a loser's excuse for a winner's position.

Lazy people want much but get little, while the diligent are prospering.
Proverbs 13:4 (TLB)

During the reign of Abdullah the Third, a great drought struck Baghdad. The Mohammedan doctors issued a decree that all the faithful should offer prayers for rain. Still, the drought continued.

The Jews were then permitted to add their prayers. Their supplications also appeared ineffectual. Finally when the drought resulted in widespread famine, the Christians in the land were asked to pray. It so happened that torrents of rain followed almost immediately.

The whole *Conclave* was more upset over the cessation of the drought than it had been alarmed at its continuance. Feeling that some explanation was necessary, they issued this statement to the masses: 'The God of our Prophet was highly gratified by the prayers of the faithful which were as sweet-smelling savours to Him. He refused their requests in order to prolong the pleasure of listening to their prayers; but the prayers of those Christian infidels were an abomination to Him, and He granted their petitions the sooner to be rid of their loathsome importunities.'

Be careful how you ridicule a victor. He may have the skill to best you again in yet another contest.

Do the thing you fear and the death of fear is certain.

Be strong and of good courage, do not fear nor be afraid of them; for the LORD your God, He is the One who goes with you. He will not leave you nor forsake you.
Deuteronomy 31:6 (NKJ)

On a summer morning as he was fixing his breakfast, Ray Blankenship looked out of his window to see a young girl being swept along in the rain-flooded drainage ditch beside his Ohio home. Blankenship knew that farther downstream, the ditch disappeared with a roar underneath the road and then emptied into the main culvert.

Ray dashed from his home and raced along the ditch, trying to get ahead of the flailing child. Finally, he hurled himself into the deep, churning water. When he surfaced, he was able to grab the girl's arm. The two tumbled head over heels and then, within about three feet of the yawning culvert, Ray's free hand felt something protrude from the bank. He clung to it desperately, the tremendous force of the water trying to tear him and the child away.

By the time fire-department rescuers arrived, Blankenship amazingly had pulled the girl to safety. Both were treated for shock. In that heroic moment, Ray Blankenship was at even greater risk than most people knew . . . since . . . Ray couldn't swim.

Today, let your courage respond to needs that you see, not to fear you may feel.

God plus one is always a majority!

If God be for us,
who can be against us?
Romans 8:31 (AV)

Wishing to encourage her young son's progress at the piano, a mother bought tickets to an Ignace Paderewski performance. When the night arrived, the two found their seats near the front of the concert hall. The boy stared in wide-eyed amazement at the majestic grand piano on the stage. The mother began talking to a friend sitting nearby and she failed to notice her son slip away. As the house lights dimmed and the spotlight lit the piano, the woman gasped as she saw her son at the piano stool, innocently picking out 'Twinkle, Twinkle, Little Star'.

Before the woman could retrieve her son, the famous concert pianist appeared on stage and quickly moved to the keyboard. 'Don't stop – keep playing,' he whispered to the boy. Leaning over, Paderewski reached down with his left hand and began filling in a bass part. Then with his right arm, he reached around the other side, encircling the child, to add a running obligato. Together, the old master and the young novice mesmerised the crowd.

No matter how insignificant, or 'amateurish' you may feel today, the Master has these words for you, 'Don't stop – keep playing,' He will add whatever is needed to turn your efforts into a masterpiece.

Whoever gossips to you will
be a gossip of you.

A gossip betrays a confidence,
but a trustworthy man keeps a secret.
Proverbs 11:13 (NIV)

In 1752, a group of Methodist men, including John Wesley, signed a covenant which every man agreed to hang on his study wall. The six articles of this solemn agreement were as follows:

1. That we will not listen to or willingly inquire after ill concerning one another;
2. That, if we do hear any ill of each other, we will not be forward to believe it;
3. That as soon as possible we will communicate what we hear by speaking or writing to the person concerned;
4. That until we have done this, we will not write or speak a syllable of it to any other person;
5. That neither will we mention it, after we have done this, to any other person;
6. That we will not make any exception to any of these rules unless we think ourselves absolutely obliged in conference.

Talk about an Anti-Gossip Pact!

Always remember: the person who tells you 'don't tell this to a soul' has probably told all the souls you know.

Jesus is a friend who knows all your faults and still loves you anyway.

Yet the proof of God's amazing love is this: that it is while we were sinners that Christ died for us.
Romans 5:8 (JBP)

Matthew was a tax collector, a hated man among the Jews for helping Rome tighten its occupation. Even so . . . Jesus loved Matthew, and eventually chose him as one of His apostles.

Peter had a quick temper, his emotions easily triggered by circumstances. He denied knowing Jesus three times during the most critical hours of Jesus' life on earth. Even so . . . Jesus loved Peter and empowered him to lead the early church.

Saul 'made havoc' of the church in Jerusalem, leading raids on the homes of Christians and imprisoning the devout. He consented to the death of Stephen, and was one of the official witnesses of his execution. He even requested letters of authority to extend the persecution of the church to other cities, including Damascus. Even so . . . Jesus loved Saul, appeared to him in a light from Heaven, and called him to repentance.

No matter what a person may have done – no matter their character flaws – Jesus loves them. He loved them to the point of dying on their behalf on the Cross . . . including dying for your enemy . . . the friend or family member who disappoints you or frustrates you . . . indeed, including *you*.

Every person should have a special cemetery lot in which to bury the faults of friends and loved ones.

And be kind to one another, tender-hearted, forgiving one another, even as God in Christ forgave you.
Ephesians 4:32 (NKJ)

An old legend tells of a covey of quail that lived in a forest. They would have been happy except for their enemy, the quail catcher. He would imitate their call, and then when they gathered together, he would throw a net over them, stuff them into his hunting basket, and carry them off to market.

One wise quail said, 'Brothers, I have a plan. When the hunter puts his net over us, we each should put our head into a section of the net and begin to flap our wings. We can lift the net together and fly away with it.' All agreed. The next day, they did just that, making a successful escape. After several days, the hunter's wife asked him, 'Where are the quail to take to market?' He replied, 'The trouble is that all the birds work together and help one another escape.'

A while later, one quail began to fight with another. 'I lifted all the weight on the net. You didn't help at all,' he cried. The other quail became angry and before long, the entire covey was quarrelling. The hunter saw his chance. He imitated the cry of the quail and cast his net over them. Preoccupied with their quarrelling, they didn't help one another and lift the net in flight. Sometimes pointing out the fault of others can 'do us in' as well.

Ignorance is always swift to speak.

Let every man be swift to hear,
slow to speak, slow to wrath.
James 1:19 (AV)

One of the favourite stories of Arturo Toscanini, the great symphony conductor, was this:

An orchestra was playing Beethoven's *Leonore* overture, which has two great musical climaxes. Each of these musical high points is followed by a trumpet passage, which the composer intended to be played offstage.

The first climax arrived, but no sound came from a trumpet offstage. The conductor, annoyed, went on to the second musical high point. But again – no trumpet could be heard.

This time, the conductor rushed into the wings, fuming and with every intent of demanding a full explanation. There he found the trumpet player struggling with the house security man who was insisting as he held for dear life onto the man's trumpet, 'I tell you, you can't play that trumpet back here! You'll disturb the rehearsal!'

Until you know *why* someone is acting the way they do, it's better not to criticise them. Until you know who has told him to act, it's better not to attempt to stop him!

Learn from other's mistakes rather than making them all yourself.

The way of a fool seems right to him, but a wise man listens to advice.
Proverbs 12:15 (NIV)

In his autobiography, Lee Iacocca gives others an opportunity to learn from a mistake he once made. In 1956, Ford emphasised car safety rather than performance and horsepower. The company introduced crash padding for dashboards and sent out a film to explain how much safer the new dashboards were. The narrator on the film claimed the padding was so thick a person could drop an egg on it from a two-storey building and it would bounce right off without breaking. As a district assistant manager for Ford, Iacocca decided he'd demonstrate this fact.

With 1,100 salesmen watching him, he climbed a high ladder and proceeded to drop an egg on a strip of the dash padding he had placed on the floor of the stage. The egg missed the padding and splattered on the floor. A second egg bounced off his assistant's shoulder. Eggs three and four landed on target, but broke on impact. Finally, with the fifth egg, he got the desired result. Iacocca writes, 'I learned two lessons that day. First, never use eggs at a sales rally. And second, never go before our customers without rehearsing what you want to say – as well as what you're going to *do* – to help sell your product.'

Good advice!

Pick your friends
but not to pieces.

*Like a club or a sword or a sharp arrow
is the man who gives false testimony
against his neighbour.*
Proverbs 25:18 (NIV)

A trumpeter was once captured by the enemy. He pleaded with his captors: 'Please spare me! I have no gun, I am not guilty of any crime. I have not killed a single one of your soldiers. I only carry this poor brass trumpet and play it when I'm told to.'

'That is the very reason for putting you to death,' his captors said. 'For, while you do not fight yourself, your trumpet stirs up all the others to battle. It causes many others to kill!'

So it is with our criticisms of others. We may not hate, mistrust or avoid the person we criticise, but our criticism can cause others to manifest these feelings and behaviours.

There once was a woman to whom gossip and criticism were so utterly distasteful that whenever a visitor brought up something negative about a person, she would say, 'Come, let's go and ask if this is true.' The talebearer was always so taken aback that he or she would beg to be excused. But the determined woman would insist on escorting the reluctant soul to the subject of the tale to verify its truth or to hear the other point of view. After a while, no one repeated a tale or voiced a criticism in her presence!

Build up your friends . . . don't tear them down!

He who throws dirt loses ground.

Stop lying to each other; tell the truth, for we are parts of each other and when we lie to each other we are hurting ourselves.
Ephesians 4:25 (TLB)

The outstanding Christian businessman, R. G. LeTourneau, after whom LeTourneau College was named, made a fortune with a company that manufactured large earthmoving equipment. He once remarked, 'We used to make a scraper known as "Model G". One day somebody asked our salesman what the G stood for. The man, who was pretty quick on the trigger, immediately replied, "I'll tell you. The G stands for gossip because like a talebearer this machine moves a lot of dirt and moves it fast." '

The trouble with gossip is not so much that it is spoken as an intended lie, but that it is *heard* as if it was the absolute truth. Abraham Lincoln had a favourite riddle he used to put to people: 'If a man were to call the tail of a dog a leg, how many legs would the dog have?'

The usual reply was 'five'.

'Wrong,' Lincoln would say with his wry smile. 'The dog still has four legs. Calling the tail a leg doesn't make it one.'

Just because a tale may have been repeated many times by so-called 'reliable sources' doesn't necessarily make it true.

You don't have to lie awake
nights to succeed – just stay
awake days.

*As long as it is day, we must do the work
of him who sent me. Night is coming,
when no-one can work.*
John 9:4 (NIV)

Entrepreneur Victor Kiam, perhaps most famous for promoting electric razors in recent years, once worked as a salesman for Lever Brothers. If he was going to be selling in a particular town, Kiam liked to arrive there the night before so he could get a good night's sleep and start his appointments early. If he couldn't find a hotel room, he'd sleep in his car.

On one of his trips to Baton Rouge, he arrived at 1.00 am and found no room at any inn. He parked on the side of a country road and flopped into the back seat. At about 3.00 am he was awakened by a policeman knocking on the car window. He told the policeman what he was doing and found him very sympathetic. 'If anything happened to you I wouldn't forgive myself,' the policeman said. 'I'll tell you what. Why don't you come down to the jailhouse and sleep in one of the cells? You can get up and go as soon as you wake up.'

And so Kiam spent the night in an unlocked cell. The next morning the policeman treated him to coffee, ham and eggs, and a sweet roll. He says, 'They ran a very nice establishment. I liked the place so much I wished I could have bought it.'

Kiam was not only was willing to work long days, but also was clever in making his 'nights' work *for* him!

The first step to wisdom is silence; the second is listening.

Let the wise listen and
add to their learning,
and let the discerning get guidance.
Proverbs 1:5 (NIV)

Helen Keller was left deaf and blind by an incurable childhood illness. A patient and persistent teacher, Anne Sullivan, taught her to read through her senses of touch, smell and taste.

At the close of her autobiography Helen Keller writes:

> Fate – silent, pitiless – bars the way. Fain would I question his imperious decree; for my heart is undisciplined and passionate, but my tongue will not utter the bitter, futile words that rise to my lips, and they fall back into my heart like unshed tears. Silence sits immense upon my soul. Then comes hope with a smile and whispers, 'There is joy in self-forgetfulness.' So I try to make the light in other people's eyes my sun, the music in others' ears my symphony, the smile on others' lips my happiness.

Silence can be used to nurture pouting, anger and hatred. Far better uses for silence are reflecting, meditating and listening. It is only when we are truly silent before the Lord that we can hear His still small voice speaking in our souls.

The greatest possession you have is the 24 hours directly in front of you.

. . . For there is a time there for every purpose and for every work.
Ecclesiastes 3:17 (AV)

Dr C. C. Albertson once wrote this about the use of time: 'It might be wise for us to take a little inventory of our resources as to time and review our habits for using it. There are 168 hours in each week. Fifty-six of these we spend in sleep. Of the remaining 112 hours, we devote 48 to labour. This leaves 64 hours, of which let us assign 12 hours for our daily meals . . .

'We have left 52 hours, net, of conscious active life to devote to any purpose to which we are inclined.

'Is it too much to say that God requires a tithe of this free time? One tenth of 52 hours is 5.2 hours. How much of this tithe of time do we devote to strictly religious uses?'

If one allowed an hour for church and an hour for a Bible study or prayer meeting each week, we would still have 192 minutes a week – enough for nearly a half hour each day in prayer and Bible reading. Such a person would still have more than 45 hours a week for life's chores and personal fun!

The old excuse, 'I have too little time,' doesn't fly. What is more likely the case is this: too little planning of the time we have!

The most valuable gift you can give another is a good example.

For I have given you an example, that you also should do as I have done to you.
John 13:15 (RSV)

In his autobiography, Armand Hammer – known as much for his humanitarian efforts as for being chairman and CEO of Occidental Petroleum, an advisor to presidents from Roosevelt to Reagan, and an industrialist – reveals the roots of his giving spirit:

'My father had become a prominent and greatly loved figure in the area . . . it was an almost ecstatic experience for me to ride with him when he went on his doctor's rounds . . . patients at their doors greeted him with such warmth that waves of pride and honour would surge in me to find myself the son of such a father, a man so obviously good, so obviously deserving of the affection he received.

'He could have made himself many times richer, however, if he had insisted on collecting all his bills; or if he could have restrained himself from giving money away; but then he would not have been the man he was . . . I have seen, in his office, drawers full of unpaid bills for which he refused to demand payment because he knew the difficult circumstances of the patients. And I heard innumerable stories from patients about his leaving money behind to pay for the prescriptions he had written when he visited people who were too poor to eat, let alone pay the doctor.'

What a wonderful legacy to leave your child – the 'business' of loving and giving to others.

Don't be afraid of pressure. Remember that pressure is what turns a lump of coal into a diamond.

You know that the testing of your faith develops perseverance. Perseverance must finish its work so that you may be mature and complete, not lacking anything.
James 1:3,4 (NIV)

An old legend says that God first created birds without wings. Sometime later, God made wings and said to the birds, 'Come, take up these burdens and bear them.' The birds hesitated at first, but soon obeyed. They tried picking up the wings in their beaks, but found them too heavy. Then they tried picking them up with their claws, but found them too large. Finally one of the birds managed to get the wings hoisted onto its shoulders where it was finally possible to carry them.

To the amazement of the birds, before long the wings began to grow and they soon had attached themselves to the bodies of the birds. One of the birds began to flap his wings and others followed his example. Shortly afterwards, one of the birds took off and began to soar in the air above

What had once been a heavy burden now became the very thing that enabled the birds to go where they could never go before . . . and at the same time, truly fulfil the destiny of their creation.

The duties and responsibilities you count as burdens today may be part of God's destiny for your life, the means by which your soul is lifted up and prepared for eternity.

A minute of thought is worth more than an hour of talk.

Set a watch, O Lord, before my mouth;
keep the door of my lips.
Psalm 141:3 (AV)

When William Gladstone was Chancellor of the Exchequer, he once requested that the Treasury send him certain statistics upon which he might base his budget proposals. The statistician made a mistake. But Gladstone was so certain of this man's concern for accuracy that he didn't take the time to verify the figures. As a result, he went before the House of Commons and made a speech based upon the incorrect figures given to him. His speech was no sooner published than the inaccuracies were exposed and Gladstone became the brunt of public ridicule.

The Chancellor sent for the statistician who had given him the erroneous information. The man arrived full of fear and shame, certain he was going to be dismissed. Instead, Gladstone said, 'I know how much you must be disturbed over what has happened, and I have sent for you to put you at your ease. For a long time you have been engaged in handling the intricacies of the national accounts, and this is the first mistake that you have made. I want to congratulate you, and express to you my keen appreciation.'

It takes a big person to extend mercy . . . a big person to listen rather than talk . . . a big person to think before jumping into action.

You can win more friends
with your ears than with
your mouth.

*Let every man be swift to hear, slow to
speak, slow to wrath.*
James 1:19 (AV)

Rabbi Harold S. Kushner writes in *When All You've Ever Wanted Isn't Enough:*

'A business associate of my father's died under particularly tragic circumstances, and I accompanied my father to the funeral. The man's widow and children were surrounded by clergy and psychiatrists trying to ease their grief and make them feel better. They knew all the right words, but nothing helped. They were beyond being comforted. The widow kept saying, "You're right, I know you're right but it doesn't make any difference." Then a man walked in, a big burly man in his eighties who was a legend in the toy and game industry. He had come to the United States illiterate and penniless and had built up an immensely successful company. He was known as a hard bargainer, a ruthless competitor. Despite his success, he had never learned to read or write . . . He had been sick recently, and his face and his walking showed it. But he walked over to the widow and started to cry, and she cried with him, and you could feel the atmosphere in the room change. This man who had never read a book in his life spoke the language of the heart and held the key that opened the gates of solace where learned doctors and clergy could not.'

It's not the outlook but the uplook that counts.

Looking unto Jesus the author and finisher of our faith . . .
Hebrews 12:2 (AV)

A twelve-year-old boy accepted Jesus Christ as his personal Saviour and Lord during a weekend revival meeting. The next week his school friends questioned him about the experience.

'Did you hear God talk?' one asked.

'No,' the boy said.

'Did you have a vision?' another asked.

'No,' the boy replied.

'Well how did you know it was God?' a third friend asked.

The boy thought for a moment and then said, 'It's like when you catch a fish. You can't see the fish or hear the fish; you just feel him tugging on your line. I felt God tugging on my heart.'

So often we try to figure out life by what we can see, hear or experience with our other senses. We make calculated estimates and judgements based on empirical evidence. There's a level of truth, however, that cannot be perceived by the senses or measured objectively. It's at that level where faith abounds. It is our faith that compels us to believe, even when we cannot explain to others why or how or to what specific earthly end. By our faith we only know in Whom we trust. And that is sufficient.

Put others before yourself,
and you can become a
leader among men.

It shall not be so among you; but whoever
would be great among you must be your
servant, and whoever would be first
among you must be your slave.
Matthew 20:26,27 (RSV)

The following set of contrasting remarks has been offered as a character sketch of a good leader. For a personal challenge, as you read through the list, circle the descriptive words you believe most closely identify you!

Self-reliant but not Self-sufficient
Energetic but not Self-seeking
Steadfast but not Stubborn
Tactful but not Timid
Serious but not Sullen
Loyal but not Sectarian
Unmovable but not Stationary
Gentle but not Hypersensitive
Tender-hearted but not Touchy
Conscientious but not a Perfectionist
Disciplined but not Demanding
Generous but not Gullible
Meek but not Weak
Humorous but not Hilarious
Friendly but not Familiar
Holy but not Holier-than-thou
Discerning but not Critical
Progressive but not Pretentious
Authoritative but not Autocratic

Ask God to help you develop in the descriptive words you didn't circle.

Feed your faith and your doubts will starve to death.

*But we are not of those who shrink back
and are destroyed, but of those who
believe and are saved .*
Hebrews 10:39 (NIV)

Richard E. Byrd spent the winter of 1934 at Bolling Advance Weather Base in Antarctica, where the temperature ranged from –58° to –76°. By the time he was rescued, he was suffering from frostbite and carbon monoxide poisoning. He wrote in his book, *Alone*, 'I had hardly strength to move. I clung to the sleeping bag, which was the only source of comfort and warmth left to me and mournfully debated the little that might be done. Two facts stood clear. One was that my chances of recovering were slim. The other was that in my weakness I was incapable of taking care of myself. *But you must have faith – you must have faith in the outcome,* I whispered to myself. It is like a flight . . . into another unknown. You start and you cannot turn back. You must go on . . . trusting your instruments, the course you have plotted.'

With faith as his only guidance system, Byrd forced himself to do the necessary things for survival *very slowly* and with *great deliberation*. At times he felt as if he were living a thousand years in any given minute. But at each day's end, he could say he was still alive. And that was enough.

Sometimes the only thing left to do in a situation is to press on in faith. And so . . . press on!

Never pass up a chance to
keep your mouth shut.

Even a fool is thought wise
if he keeps silent, and discerning
if he holds his tongue.
Proverbs 17:28 (NIV)

President Calvin Coolidge, the thirtieth president of the United States, was a reserved man who spoke very little. A reporter attempted to interview him, and the conversation went as follows:

Reporter: Do you wish to say anything about the war threat in Europe?

Coolidge: No.

Reporter: About the strike in the clothing factories?

Coolidge: No.

Reporter: About the League of Nations?

Coolidge: No.

Reporter: About the farm production problem?

Coolidge: No.

As the reporter began to leave the room, Coolidge unexpectedly called him back and said, 'Don't quote me.'

Never let yourself feel pressurised into saying something you don't want to say, or into saying something when you don't feel like talking. Silence is not a 'lack' of communication. It is a form of communication, and it can be a very effective one at that.

It isn't hard to make a mountain out of a molehill. Just add a little dirt.

Starting a quarrel is like breaching a dam;
so drop the matter before a dispute
breaks out.
Proverbs 17:14 (NIV)

The story is told of a boy and his mother who went to a shopping centre. The boy acted badly – demanding this and that, running away from his mother, hiding so she couldn't find him, whining that he wanted something to eat or drink, interrupting her while she was attempting to talk to salesmen or buy something. In total exasperation, she finally gave up and returned to the car.

As they were driving home, the boy could sense her displeasure and he said, 'I learned last week in Sunday school that when we ask God to forgive us when we are bad, He does. Does He really do that?'

The mother replied, 'Yes, He does.' The boy continued, 'And the teacher said that when He forgives us, He throws our sins in the deepest sea. Does He do that, mum?' The mother responded, 'Yes, that's what the Bible says.'

The boy was silent for a moment and then he said, 'I've asked God to forgive me for acting bad at the shops, but I bet when we get home, you're going to go fishing for those sins, aren't you?'

Surely one of the best ways to avoid a quarrel with a person is to avoid going fishing for their past sins!

What counts is not the number of hours you put in, but how much you put in the hours.

Whatever your hand finds to do, do it with your might . . .
Ecclesiastes 9:10 (RSV)

In 1930, Pat O'Brien had a scene in a play *The Up and Up* in which he had to contend with two angry people at once – a person on the phone and one at his desk. To him, playing the scene was 'like fighting through Notre Dame's football line while singing "Danny Boy". The play received mixed reviews and its outlook seemed dim. O'Brien thought, *Why knock myself out on something with no future?* But then a Bible verse echoed in his memory; 'Whatever task likes to your hand, do it with all your might' (Ecclesiastes 9:10). And so, at every performance, he put his all into the scene, sometimes coming off stage wringing wet.

After the show closed, O'Brien went on to a few obscure parts. Then one day he received a phone call from a man who said, 'Mr Hughes is filming the play *The Front Page* and wants you in it.' O'Brien jumped at the opportunity. The film's director, Lewis Milestone, later told him why he was chosen. Milestone had gone to New York with friends, planning to see a hit show, but they were one seat short so Lewis went to see *The Up and Up*. He said, 'One scene really impressed me – the one at the desk.' O'Brien's outstanding film career was launched by his giving his all . . . for a part that had seemed worthless!

Reputation is made in a
moment: character is built
in a lifetime.

My righteousness I hold fast, and
will not let it go;
My heart shall not reproach me as
long as I live.
Job 27:6 (NKJ)

A man once had a friend who was a skilled potter. He often went to watch him at work as he moulded the clay into various vessels. One day he asked his friend how he determined what he was going to make. The potter said he had discovered that when he was rested, he tended to make beautiful things, but when he was tired, he made more ordinary vessels for menial uses. As the potter reflected on this, he concluded that when he was relaxed, he had *both the ability to focus and the patience* to make something beautiful. Often the process of making a perfect object involved crushing an almost completed vase or bowl back into a lump so that he might start again. Beautiful objects also required that he be much more careful at each stage. When he was tired, by contrast, he was less able to focus, less patient, and thus more apt to make mistakes and more likely to resort to making items that did not demand such precision.

So it is with our lives. Building character takes focus and patience, with attention to detail and an ability to be consistent over time. While God is ultimately our Potter, we also play the role of potter in forming our own character. The more stressed we are, the less likely we are to create a character of beauty.

If you feel 'dog tired' at night, maybe it's because you 'growled' all day.

If it is possible, as far as it depends on you, live at peace with everyone.
Romans 12:18 (NIV)

General Horace Porter once wrote about a conversation he had with General Ulysses Grant one evening while they were sitting by a campfire. Porter noted, 'General, it seems singular that you should have gone through all the rough and tumble of army service and frontier life, and have never been provoked into swearing. I have never heard you utter an oath.'

Grant replied, 'Well, somehow or other, I never learned to swear. When I was a boy I seemed to have an aversion to it, and when I became a man I saw the folly of it. I have always noticed, too, that swearing helps to arouse a man's anger; and when a man flies into a passion his adversary who keeps cool always gets the better of him. In fact, I could never see the value of swearing. I think it is the case with many people who swear excessively that it is a mere habit . . . they do not mean to be profane; to say the least, it is a great waste of time.'

Not only does anger give rise to harsh words, but harsh words feed anger. The seething soul uses up valuable inner energy, leaving far less for the normal healthy functioning of spirit, mind and body. To rid yourself of feelings of anger and frustration, perhaps the first step is to watch your tongue!

If you don't want the fruits of sin, stay out of the devil's orchard.

Steer clear of evil in any form.
1 Thessalonians 5:22 (JBP)

As college roommates, Meg and Ann also became best friends. Then one day, Meg told Ann that John had asked her for a date. Ann was disappointed; she'd had a crush on John for two years. Still, she managed to say, 'Have a good time' and later, to put on a happy face at John and Meg's wedding.

Through the years, Meg kept the relationship with Ann close. Ann enjoyed teasing and laughing with John. When Meg asked Ann to join them at a beach-side bungalow for a week, Ann jumped at the chance. On an afternoon when Meg went out to visit a friend, Ann and John betrayed Meg's trust. Afterwards, Ann felt sick inside. Deep shame welled up in her.

A few minutes of flirtation and passion resulted in more than a decade of misery for Ann. She might never have known happiness again if Meg hadn't confronted her about her refusal to accept a marriage proposal. Ann sobbed, 'I'm horrible. You don't know how I've wronged you.' Meg said, 'I do know, Ann,' and one look into her eyes confirmed that Meg had known, had loved and had forgiven. With that forgiveness, years of shameful pain melted away – pain that could have been avoided by a few right choices easily made at the 'beginning' of temptation.

Our children are like mirrors – they reflect our attitudes in life.

The righteous man leads a blameless life:
blessed are his children after him.
Proverbs 20:7 (NIV)

A man was asked to give a commencement address several years ago and as he sat on the platform after the speech watching the graduates receive their college degrees, the entire audience began applauding for a student who had earned a perfect 4.0 grade point average. During the applause, a faculty member seated next to the speaker leaned over and said to him, 'She may be Miss Genius, but her attitude stinks.' The speaker later said, 'Without even thinking, my hands stopped clapping for her in mid-air. I couldn't help but think, *How sad.*'

No matter how beautiful, intelligent, talented or athletic a child may be . . . there's no substitute for a child having a positive, loving attitude towards others! The foremost architect of that attitude is not going to be a teacher or a pastor, but the parents.

Be careful in the attitudes you 'feed' your children daily. They become the diet of your child's mind, just as food becomes the diet for your child's body. Don't feed your children junk ideas, sour opinions, rotten theology, poison feelings or wilted enthusiasm. Instead, feed your children with the best and most positive ideas, expressions of feeling and opinions you have!

The art of being a good
guest is knowing when to
leave.

*Let your foot be seldom in your
neighbour's house,*
lest he become weary of you and hate you.
Proverbs 25:17 (RSV)

A man and his wife once met a young couple about their age during a welcome meeting after church. The next Sunday when they spotted the newcomers again, they invited them to their home for coffee after the Sunday evening service. The newcomers happily accepted their invitation.

Both the conversation and coffee were warm and cosy, but the evening began to grow long. Still, the young couple – perhaps overly eager to make friends – talked on and on about their move to the city, the learning curve they were experiencing in their new jobs, the difficulty they had settling their children into new schools, their long search for a church, the trials of finding a dentist, doctor, shoe repairman and dry cleaners.

No matter how many times the host and hostess yawned or failed to reply, the couple had more to say. Finally, even the visiting couple began to yawn. Still, they made no motion towards leaving.

At long last, the host stood to his feet and with a wide stretch of his arms, he looked at his wife and said, 'Well, darling, let's go up to bed so these nice people can go home!'

Your chances of being asked back are better when you don't wear out your welcome.

He who cannot forgive
breaks the bridge over
which he himself must pass.

*Your heavenly Father will forgive you if
you forgive those who sin against you.*
Matthew 6:14 (TLB)

One Sunday afternoon, Doris Louise Seger opened the door of her church office to practise a violin solo she was to play that night, only to find her violin in pieces, scattered across the floor. Doris was crushed. She had received the violin fifty years earlier as a high school graduation present from her parents. She thought, *Who? Why? How can I forgive that person?*

A week later police found the vandal and Doris went to his home. When she saw the skinny, blond 11-year-old sitting next to his father, she understood that the real tragedy was not her shattered violin, but a young life that seemed headed for a shattered future. She explained to the family what the violin had meant to her life and then she found herself saying, 'I forgive you, and God will, too, if you ask Him.'

A few days later, the boy came to the pastor's office, asking hesitantly, 'Is there any work that I can do at the church to pay for the violin?' At the sign of his repentant heart, the pastor shared the gospel with him and the boy received Jesus as his Saviour that day.

Doris purchased a new violin, but as she later wrote. 'It would never compare with this "new creature" in Christ Jesus. I learned anew that God's grace is sufficient to give me a forgiving heart.'

Jesus is a friend who walks in when the world has walked out.

I have told you these things, so that in me you may have peace. In this world you will have trouble. But take heart! I have overcome the world.
John 16:33 (NIV)

Babe Ruth hit 714 home runs during his baseball career, but on this particular day towards the end of his career, the Braves were playing the Reds in Cincinnati, and the great Bambino was no hero. He fumbled the ball and threw badly. In one innings alone, his errors were responsible for most of the five runs scored by Cincinnati.

As the Babe walked off the field and headed towards the dugout after the third out, a crescendo of angry cries and boos rose to greet him. Then . . . a boy jumped over the railing and ran out onto the field. With tears streaming down his face, he threw his arms around the legs of his hero.

Ruth didn't hesitate for a second. He picked up the boy, hugged him, then set him down and patted his head. The cries from the crowd abruptly stopped. A hush fell over the entire park. In that brief moment, the fans saw two heroes on the field: Ruth, who in spite of his own dismal day in fielding, cared about the feelings of a young fan; and a small boy, who cared about the feelings of another human being.

No matter what your performance on the playing field of life is today, the Lord has a hug waiting for you at the day's end. He is your Number One Fan.

Those who deserve love
the least
need it the most.

But I say to you, love your enemies, bless those who curse you, do good to those who hate you, and pray for those who spitefully use you and persecute you.
Matthew 5:44 (NKJ)

When Mrs Booth, whose husband founded the Salvation Army, was just a girl, she was running by the road one day with her hoop and stick when she saw a prisoner being dragged by a constable to the city jail. A mob had gathered to hoot at the culprit, who walked with his head hung low – the picture of guilt and shame. His image of utter loneliness tugged at her heart. It seemed to her that he didn't have a friend in the entire world. She quickly sprang to his side and marched, head high and a smile on her face, all the way to the prison with him. She was determined to let him know that, guilty or not, there was at least one soul that felt compassion for him.

Too often we are willing to let a 'guilty party' take the full brunt of their punishment, or wallow in their misery, without comfort or words of consolation and encouragement. The issue may not be crime but may be divorce or estrangement. The best way to restore a person to a relationship with both God and the offended party, however, is not to let the person remain alone to become fearful or bitter – but rather, to reach out in love and provide support. This does not mean that you condone the action. It does mean that you refuse to condemn the person!

Faith is daring the soul to go
beyond what the eyes
can see.

For we walk by faith, not by sight.
2 Corinthians 5:7 (AV)

During his two years in the army, David Brenner made the most of his posting to Europe by travelling at every opportunity. To heighten his sense of excitement, he often showed up at a railway station and bought a ticket to wherever the next train was going.

One day he bought a ticket for Rome and since the train was scheduled to leave immediately, he raced across the station, but still arrived at the platform just as the train was pulling away. He chased after it as fast as he could run! Standing on the platform of the last carriage was a well-dressed man who motioned for him to hand him his bags. He quickly tossed him his smaller bag and then his larger suitcase. By this time, he was growing weary from running, but then he looked into the man's face! The smirk he saw quickly told him that the man had offered his help not altruistically, but criminally. If Brenner didn't make it on board, this man had brand-new clothes and gear!

Brenner kicked up his heels and, running as never before, he managed to grab the railing by the entrance to the last carriage. With all the strength he could muster, he swung himself aboard.

Adversity sometimes comes to rob you. Instead, let it motiviate your faith to be even *more* daring!

The right angle to approach a difficult problem is the 'try-angle'.

For nothing is impossible with God.
Luke 1:37 (NIV)

Many years ago, a huge oil refinery caught fire. Flames shot hundreds of feet into the air and the sky filled with grimy smoke. The heat was so intense that firemen parked a few roads away, hoping for the heat to die down. Instead, the fire raged ever closer to a nearby row of tanks.

Suddenly, a fire engine came careering down the street. With its brakes screeching, it hit the kerb directly in front of the blaze. The firemen jumped out and began to battle the blaze. Inspired by this act, the other firemen drove closer and joined in the fight. As a result of their co-operative effort, the fire was brought under control in the nick of time.

Those who witnessed these events decided to honour the man who had driven the lead fire engine to the brink of the blaze. In preparing for the awards ceremony, the mayor said, 'Captain, we want to honour you for your fantastic act. You prevented the loss of property, perhaps even the loss of life. Is there something we can give you as a token of our appreciation?' The captain replied without hesitation, 'Your Honour, a new set of brakes would be dandy!'

Acts of heroism all begin the same way: one person is willing to try when all the others are not.

The fellow who does things
that count doesn't usually
stop to count them.

*Brothers, I do not consider myself yet to
have taken hold of it. But one thing I do:
Forgetting what is behind and straining
towards what is ahead . . .*
Philippians 3:13 (NIV)

For more than a quarter of a century, Arnold Billie was a rural mail carrier in southern New Jersey. His daily route took him sixty-three miles through two counties and five municipalities. Mr Billie, as he was affectionately known, did more than deliver the mail. He provided 'personal service'. Anything a person might need to buy from the post office, Mr Billie provided – stamps, money orders, pickup service. All a customer needed to do was leave the flag up on their mailbox.

One elderly woman had trouble starting her lawn mower, so whenever she wanted to use it, she would simply leave it by her mailbox, raise the flag, and when Mr Billie came by, he would start it for her! Mr Billie gave a new definition to the phrase 'public servant'.

True Christian servants rarely think of themselves as doing anything other than the ordinary, when what they actually do is quite extraordinary! The apostle Paul called himself a *slave* to Christ, yet he was more concerned about being a good servant to ever worry about being a real slave. Why? Because true servants are motivated by love. It is love they know they have received from Christ. And it is love they give.

A critical spirit is like poison ivy – it only takes a little contact to spread its poison.

But avoid worldly and empty chatter, for it will lead to further ungodliness, and their talk will spread like gangrene . . .
2 Timothy 2:16,17 (NASB)

Glenn Van Ekeren tells about an experience he had with his son one summer holiday. For the first couple of days, his son Matt seemed to misbehave constantly. Glenn seemed to be continually rebuking and correcting him. Thinking, *No son of mine is going to act this way*, he made it clear to his son in no uncertain terms that he expected him to start behaving.

Matt tried very hard to live up to his father's standards. In fact, a day went by later in the week in which he hadn't done a single thing that called for correcting. That night, after Matt had said his prayers and jumped into bed, Glenn noticed that Matt's bottom lip began to quiver. 'What's the matter, buddy?' he asked his son. Barely able to speak, Matt looked up at his father with tear-filled eyes and asked, 'Daddy, haven't I been a good boy today?'

Glenn said, 'Those words cut through my parental arrogance like a knife. I had been quick to criticise and correct his misbehaviour, but failed to mention my pleasure with his attempt to be a good boy. My son taught me never to put my children to bed without a word of appreciation and encouragement.'

Laziness and poverty are cousins.

A little sleep, a little slumber,
a little folding of the hands to rest –
and poverty will come on you
like a bandit
and scarcity like an armed man.
Proverbs 24:33,34 (NIV)

One day, a grandfather told his grandchildren about his coming to America. He told of the trains and ships that he took from his home in Eastern Europe. He told of being processed at Ellis Island and how he had gone to a cafeteria in lower Manhattan to get something to eat. There, he sat down at an empty table and waited quite some time for someone to take his order. Nobody came. Finally, a woman with a tray full of food sat down opposite him and explained to him how a cafeteria works.

She said, 'You start at that end' – pointing toward a stack of trays – 'and then go along the food line and pick out what you want. At the other end, they'll tell you how much you have to pay.'

The grandfather reflected a moment and then said, 'I soon learned that's how everything works in America. Life's a cafeteria here. You can get anything you want – even very great success – if you are willing to pay the price. But you'll never get what you want if you wait for someone to bring it to you. You have to get up and get it yourself.'

The difference between where you are and where you want to be can often be summed up in one word: work.

Language is the expression of thought. Every time you speak, your mind is on parade.

The good man out of the good treasure of his heart produces good,
and the evil man out of his evil treasure produces evil;
for out of the abundance of the heart his mouth speaks.
Luke 6:45 (RSV)

A woman was visiting her brother and his family one time when her nephew suddenly stopped in the midst of his play and steadily gazed up at her. 'What are you thinking about?' she asked him. 'You're a Christian, auntie, aren't you?' he finally asked.

'I hope so, dear,' she replied. 'But you never talk about Jesus,' he said. 'If you loved Him *very much*, wouldn't you talk about Him sometimes?'

The aunt, taken aback a bit, stammered a reply: 'We may love a person without speaking of him,' she said.

'Can we?' her nephew asked innocently. 'I didn't know that. You talk about your papa and mamma and your brothers and sisters all the time. And you talk about other people, too – even me. But not Jesus.'

'Well, yes,' the aunt admitted, her heart quickened with conviction. 'I suppose that's been so.'

'Let's talk about Jesus sometime,' her nephew concluded before getting up to go outside to play. And then with a backward wink, he added, 'because I love Him, too, and I *like* to talk about Him.'

We talk about what – and who – matter the most to us. And what we say reveals how we feel about them.

Take care of your character
and your reputation will
take care of itself.

Take time and trouble to keep yourself
spiritually fit. Bodily fitness has a limited
value, but spiritual fitness is of unlimited
value for it holds promise both for this
present life and for the life to come.
1 Timothy 4:8 (JBP)

The first major movie star to wear a uniform in World War II was Jimmy Stewart. Unlike so many other prominent people who sought excuses not to serve, Jimmy willingly accepted the draft and tried to get into the Army Air Corps, since he already had a pilot's licence. The corps, however, had a strict weight requirement – for Jimmy's height, a minimum of 153 pounds. Stewart weighed 143. When he suggested that they forget to weigh him, the officer responded, 'That would be highly irregular.' Jimmy replied, 'Wars are highly irregular, too.' With no weighing in, Jimmy won his new role, one in which he prayed often, not for himself, but that 'I wouldn't make a mistake'.

Stewart worked his way up from buck private to fully-fledged pilot, and completed 25 missions over enemy territory, many of them as command pilot of a B-24 bomber wing. By the time he returned to Hollywood he was a full colonel with the Air Medal, Croix de Guerre, Distinguished Flying Cross, and seven battle stars. He remained in the Air Force Reserve and was promoted to brigadier general in 1959. He once said, 'There's a tremendous difference between a warmonger and a patriot.' Jimmy Stewart – though a general – was always better known as 'the nice guy'.

The hardest secret for a
man to keep is his opinion
of himself.

For I say, through the grace given to me,
to everyone who is among you,
not to think of himself more highly than
he ought to think, but to think soberly,
as God has dealt to each one
a measure of faith.
Romans 12:3 (NKJ)

A little Swiss watch had been made with the small-est of parts and great skill. It ran with precision, to the great delight of its owner. Still, the watch was dissatisfied with its restricted sphere of influence on a lady's wrist. It envied the high and lofty position of the great clock on the tower of the town hall.

One day as the little watch and its owner passed the town hall, the tiny watch exclaimed, 'I wish I could be way up there! I could serve many people instead of just one.' The watch's owner looked down and said, 'I know someone who has a key to the tower. Little watch, you shall have your opportunity!'

The next day, a slender thread was let down from the tower and the little watch was tied to it. The watch was pulled up the side of the tower – higher and higher it rose! Of course, when it reached the top, it was completely lost to view. 'Oh my,' said the watch. 'My elevation has resulted in my annihilation!'

If you desire to trade your current sphere of small influence for a larger one . . . be wary. The Lord will elevate you in His timing.

He who buries his talent is making a grave mistake.

Be sure to use the abilities God has given you . . .
1 Timothy 4:14 (TLB)

A man named Luigi Tarisio loved violins and began collecting them. He took great pride in hunting out rare finds and purchasing only those instruments that he knew to be the finest quality. No one really knew about his passion, however, until after he died. It was while his estate was being appraised that some 246 valuable violins were discovered in his attic!

One of the most expensive violins had been hidden in the drawer of an old dresser. It was a Stradivarius he had purchased from someone who had also bought it solely as a collector's item. In commenting on this, W. Y. Fullerton noted that in preserving the instrument, Tarisio had robbed the world of beautiful music all the time he treasured his violins. Others before him had done the same. In fact, by the time the greatest Stradivarius violin in his collection was finally played, 147 years had passed!

The gifts, talents, abilities and aptitudes that you have been given by the Creator are intended for you to discover and then use until they become perfect. We are to uncover who we were created to be . . . not cover up what we fear we are. Give expression to your inner self today. It is not only God's gift to you, but the very best you can ever give to others.

If a care is too small to be
turned into a prayer,
it is too small to be made
into a burden.

Casting all your care upon Him,
for He cares for you.
1 Peter 5:7 (NKJ)

Shortly after Mary Manachi's second child, Marylou, was born, she was diagnosed with Cooley's anaemia, which requires a blood transfusion every two weeks and is usually fatal before the age of 20. Assured by physicians that the genetic disorder was very rare, Mary and her husband had another baby. At six months, Rosemarie was also diagnosed with the disorder and later their son, George, was also born with Cooley's. Sadness gripped Mary and her husband.

One day, Mary walked into Rosemarie's room and found her making a beautiful pin to sell at a craft show. 'I'm going to earn all I can towards college,' she said. Then a teacher phoned to report what Rosemarie had written as the thing she was most thankful for: 'good health'! Mary took another look at her children and found them all embracing life. George was talking about becoming a geologist. Marylou was earning a place on the honour roll and practising her piano diligently. Mary finally concluded, 'If they love life so much . . . am I to love life less?'

Sometimes our burdens seem great. It helps at those times to remember those with greater burdens who carry them as 'being too small' for them even to become worries.

Even a woodpecker owes his
success to the fact that he
uses his head.

But you, keep your head in all situations . . .
2 Timothy 4:5 (NIV)

A woman was sitting in her den one day when a small black snake suddenly appeared, slithered across the floor and made its way under the couch. Being deathly afraid of snakes, the woman promptly ran to the bathroom to get her husband, who was taking a shower. He came running from the shower with only a towel around his waist, grabbed an old broom handle from the closet, and began poking under the couch.

At this point, the sleeping family dog awoke. Curious to see what was happening, he came up behind the husband and touched his cold nose to the back of the man's heel. The man, thinking that the snake had outmanoeuvred him and had bitten him on the heel, fainted dead away. The wife concluded that her husband had collapsed with a heart attack. She ran from the house to a hospital just a few streets away. The ambulance drivers promptly returned with her to the house and placed the man on a stretcher. As they were carrying him out of the house, the snake reappeared from beneath the couch. One of the drivers became so excited that he dropped his end of the stretcher and broke the husband's leg. Seeing her husband's twisted leg, the wife collapsed.

Meanwhile, the snake slithered quietly away!

The poorest of all men is not the man without a penny but the man without a dream.

Where there is no vision,
the people perish . . .
Proverbs 29:18 (AV)

An unusual band of thirteen business and professional men in Toronto, Canada, responded in a unique way to multiple-alarm fires in their city. They have formed a volunteer firefighting unit, although they don't directly fight fires. Dressed in their own rubber firefighting uniforms, they are armed with police passes. The truck they man is a red mobile canteen.

The firemen appreciate their service – in fact, the firemen's union bought the canteen truck for them, and also purchases all supplies for the truck. When a fire alarm is received, a 'must' call goes to them.

These volunteer firemen described themselves as 'middle-aged businessmen who never outgrew their childhood dreams'.

What is it that you dreamed of doing as a child?

In the most reflective moments of your life, do you still nurture that dream? Do you wonder 'what might have been if . . .'?

Dreams are not only a great source of hope and courage, they are often windows to one's destiny. Revisit your childhood dreams. Perhaps it's time for you to give them expression.

You can accomplish more in one hour with God than one lifetime without Him.

With God all things are possible.
Matthew 19:26 (AV)

Rachel and Kim owned a commercial building, half of which Jim used for his dental practice. For fifteen years, they had experienced no difficulty in renting out the other half. They counted on the extra income to pay their bills. Then they lost their tenant. An estate agent told them, 'Forget about advertising for a while. Absolutely nobody is renting.'

To ease her financial worries, Rachel started swimming laps at her local YMCA pool. One day when she was feeling especially anxious, she decided to pray as she swam, using the alphabet to keep track of the number of laps. She focused on adjectives to describe God, starting with the letter A. 'You are the *almighty* God,' she prayed on lap one. 'A *benevolent* God, a *beautiful* God,' she prayed on the next lap, and then, 'You are a *caring, creative, can-do* God.' By the time she had completed twenty-six laps, an hour had passed and her fears were gone. She knew God would provide.

A short time later, a physiotherapist called to say she had seen the 'For Rent' sign in the window and asked to see the office. It was what she wanted. So, she and her partner rented the space. Rachel still prays while swimming laps. 'After all,' she says, 'I've discovered God's goodness stretches from A to Z!'

The only preparation for tomorrow is the right use of today.

Therefore do not worry about tomorrow, for tomorrow will worry about itself. Each day has enough trouble of its own.
Matthew 6:34 (NIV)

A comic strip created by Charles Schulz addresses the need for each of us to make the most of the immediate present in our lives:

Charlie Brown is seen as bat. STRIKE THREE. He has struck out again and slumps on the players' bench. He says, 'Rats! I'll never be a big-league player. I just don't have it! All my life I've dreamed of playing in the big leagues, but I know I'll never make it.'

Lucy turns to console him. 'Charlie Brown,' she says, 'you're thinking too far ahead. What you need to do is set yourself more immediate goals.'

Charlie Brown looks up and asks, 'Immediate goals?'

Lucy responds, 'Yes. Start with this next innings when you go out to pitch. See if you can walk out to the mound without falling down.'

The first step towards walking into any future is the step you take today. Make it a forward . . . positive . . . springy and light-hearted . . . energetic . . . well-aimed . . . purposeful step. The steps you take today become the well-worn path of tomorrow.

When things go wrong, don't go wrong with them.

Do not enter the path of the wicked,
and do not walk in the way of evil men.
Proverbs 4:14 (RSV)

Medical missionary Dr Lambie, formerly of Abyssinia, forded many swift and bridgeless streams in Africa. He learned from the natives the best way to make a hazardous crossing.

The danger in crossing a stream lies in being swept off one's feet and carried downstream to deeper waters or being hurled to death against hidden rocks. A way to avoid this is for a man about to cross a stream to find a large stone, the heavier the better, to lift it to his shoulder, and carry it across the stream as ballast. The extra weight of the stone keeps his feet solid on the bed of the stream.

In telling of this technique, Dr Lambie drew an application to life: 'While crossing the dangerous stream of life . . . we need the ballast of burden-bearing . . . to keep us from being swept off our feet.'

This does not mean that we should seek out troubles or give in to our problems. Rather, it means that as we look around at others, we are to help shoulder their burdens and in return, to accept their help in bearing our own loads. It's easy to become overwhelmed in carrying only our own burden. Shared burdens, however, travel lighter.

Two things are hard on the heart – running upstairs and running down people.

Do not let any unwholesome talk come out of your mouths, but only what is helpful for building others up according to their needs, that it may benefit those who listen.
Ephesians 4:29 (NIV)

A faculty member at a university once became very distraught over the weaknesses of a particular administrator with whom he had a negative relationship. He allowed himself to think about the man constantly. Hateful, negative thoughts so preoccupied him that it affected the quality of his relationships with his family, his church and his colleagues. He finally concluded that he needed to leave and accept a teaching appointment elsewhere.

A friend asked him, 'Wouldn't you really prefer to teach at this university, if the man were not here?' 'Of course,' he responded, 'but as long as he is here, then my staying is too disruptive to everything in life. I have to go.'

The friend then asked, 'Why have you made this administrator the centre of your life?' As much as the man tried to deny the truth of this, he finally had to admit that he had allowed one individual and his weaknesses to distort his entire view of life. Still, it was not the administrator's doing. It was his own. From that day forward, he focused on his students and his teaching . . . and he found new joy in his 'old job'.

When you concentrate on running down others, usually the only one that gets run down is you.

The best way to get even is to forget.

Love your enemies! Do good to them! Lend to them! And don't be concerned about the fact that they won't repay. Then your reward from heaven will be very great, and you will truly be acting as sons of God: for he is kind to the unthankful and to those who are very wicked.

Luke 6:35 (TLB)

In his book, *Beneath the Cross of Jesus*, A. Leonard Griffith tells the story of a young Korean exchange student, a leader in Christian circles at the University of Pennsylvania, who left his apartment on the evening of April 25, 1958, to post a letter to his parents. As he turned from the mailbox, he was met by eleven leather-jacketed teenage boys. Without a word, they beat him with a cosh, a lead pipe, and their shoes and fists – and left him lying dead in the gutter.

All Philadelphia cried out for vengeance. The district attorney planned to seek the death penalty for the arrested youth. And then this letter arrived, signed by the boy's parents and twenty other relatives in Korea: 'Our family has met together and we have decided to petition that the most generous treatment possible within the laws of your government be given to those who have committed this criminal action . . . in order to give evidence of our sincere hope contained in this petition, we have decided to save money to start a fund to be used for the religious, educational, vocational and social guidance of the boys when they are released . . . We have dared to express our hope with a spirit received from the gospel of our Saviour Jesus Christ who died for our sins.'

When you forgive it takes you from the place of the victim to that of a victor.

People don't care how much
you know until they know
how much you care.

Never act from motives of rivalry or
personal vanity, but in humility think
more of each other than you do of
yourselves.
Philippians 2:3 (JBP)

Although the North American Indians had no written alphabet before they met the white man, their language was anything but primitive. The vocabulary of many Indian languages was as large as that of their French and English conquerors. Often, their expressions were far more eloquent. In an Indian tongue, for example, the concept for the word *friend* is beautifully stated as 'one-who-carries-my-sorrows-on-his-back'.

A friend or family member who comes to you for solace . . . or even claiming to be seeking advice . . . very often wants nothing more than your presence, your listening ear, and your quiet caring of sorrows. A young man discovered this shortly after his marriage. His wife frequently came home from her job telling of the woes of her day. His response was to offer suggestions and give solutions. His wife finally said to him. 'I've already solved the problems of the day.' The husband asked, perplexed, 'Then why are you telling me about them?' She replied, 'I don't need Mr Fixit. I need a loving ear.'

The friend who provides both physical and emotional shelter is a true haven, one who helps another weather a storm in safety.

Humour is to life
what shock absorbers
are to cars.

A merry heart does good, like medicine,
But a broken spirit dries the bones.
Proverbs 17:22 (NKJ)

Stand-up comedian and author David Brenner was signing books in a San Francisco bookshop when a young man handed him a newly purchased copy to be signed and said softly, 'I want to thank you for saving my life.' Brenner replied flippantly, 'That's OK.' The young man stood his ground and said, 'No, I really mean it.'

Brenner stopped signing and looked at him. The man said, 'My father died. He was my best friend. I loved him and couldn't stop crying for weeks. I decided to take my own life. The night I was going to do it, I happened to have the TV on. You were hosting *The Tonight Show*, doing your monologue. Next thing I knew I was watching you and laughing. Then I started laughing hysterically. I realised then that if I was able to laugh, I was able to live. So I want to thank you for saving my life.' Humbled and grateful, Brenner shook his hand and said, 'No, I thank *you*.'

Laughter does more than help us escape our problems. It sometimes gives us the courage to face them. As humorous author Barbara Johnson has said: 'Laughter is like changing a baby's nappy. It doesn't permanently solve any problems, but it makes things more acceptable for a while.'

A man wrapped up in
himself makes a very
small package.

*A fool finds no pleasure in understanding
but delights in airing his own opinions.*
Proverbs 18:2 (NIV)

A pompous city man, turned farmer, was showing a young boy over his property. As they drove through field after field, the man bragged incessantly about his accomplishments – how he had started from scratch as a young man and worked his way up through the business world. He told how he had earned far more money than had been necessary to buy the land and how he had invested thousands upon thousands of pounds to transform the formerly worthless farm into the agricultural paradise they were surveying. He told of the amazing yield of his crops, and the lushness of the new spring planting.

Finally, he pointed towards the stacked hay, the full granary, and the boxes of produce and declared, 'And I grew it all by myself. Started with nothing, and now look at it!'

'From nothing?' echoed the duly impressed lad.

'That's right,' said the man. 'From nothing.'

'Wow,' the young boy said, pausing to reflect for a few seconds. 'My dad farms, but he needs seeds to grow *his* crops.'

It isn't your position that makes you happy or unhappy, it's your disposition.

But godliness with contentment is great gain. For we brought nothing into this world, and it is certain we can carry nothing out.
1 Timothy 6:6,7 (AV)

A traditional Supervisor's Prayer states: 'Lord, when I am wrong, make me willing to change. When I am right, make me easy to live with. So strengthen me that the power of my example will far exceed the authority of my rank.'

A positive attitude may not directly change your circumstances but it will change the way you respond to your circumstances. The responses of positive people are far more likely to be

- active
- solution orientated
- generous towards others
- involving others
- immediate or timely
- rooted in dignity and respect

Positive people are much more likely than negative people to turn their ideas into positive behaviour. Positive behaviour, in turn, does change circumstances, and nearly always so, for the better.

Truly to grab hold of a slippery problem and rise above it, first grab hold of a positive thought!

It takes more to plough a field than merely turning it over in your mind.

Work with your hands, just as we commanded you, so that you may behave properly toward outsiders and not be in any need.
1 Thessalonians 4:11,12 (NASB)

An author, a cynical man, once sought to escape city life by moving to a little house in the country. His house was opposite a farm, and from his library window, he often looked up from his writing to watch as his neighbour engaged in a wide variety of jobs that needed to be done on his farm. He was intrigued to the point of distraction.

He watched as the man mended the fence after his cattle had broken through it. He watched as the man replanted a field after a heavy deluge washed out a new planting. He watched as he made repairs to his tractor and removed several large stones from his field after a tractor blade broke. The farmer seemed to work from sunrise to sunset, doing battle against the elements and facing one problem after another with unlimited energy. The author began to wonder about the man's optimism.

One day the author strolled from his cottage to talk to the farmer. 'You amaze me,' he said after he greeted his neighbour. 'You never seem to lose heart. Do you *always* hope for the best?'

The farmer thought for a moment and then with eyes twinkling he replied, 'No, I don't hope for it – I *hop* for it!'

Men are like fish. Neither would get into trouble if they kept their mouths shut.

He who guards his mouth and his tongue keeps himself from calamity.

Proverbs 21:23 (NIV)

Abraham Lincoln is often held up to children as a model of achievement and an embodiment of 'The American Dream'. Regarded by many as the greatest President of the United States, Lincoln's Second Inaugural Address is one of the noblest political speeches ever given, and his Gettysburg Address is still studied and memorised by many a student. Amazingly, Lincoln had only four months of formal education, and that in a one-room country schoolhouse where students ranged from age five to twenty-five. His teacher probably had no more than an eight-grade education, if that.

One day a father was reciting all of these achievements to his son. 'Where else but in America could this happen?' he mused. And then, hoping to instil in his son a little more ambition to study, he asked, 'Do you know what Abe Lincoln was doing when he was your age?'

The boy answered, 'No, but I do know what he was doing when he was your age.'

We nearly always err when we suggest to others that they be like anybody other than their own best selves. And, to our chagrin, they usually let us know we have erred!

The heart of a man
cannot be determined
by the size of his wallet.

For what will it profit a man if he gains
the whole world, and loses his own soul?
Or what will a man give in exchange for
his soul?
Mark 8:36, 37 (NKJ)

Not a lot of press coverage was given to the tough Argentine golfer Robert De Vincenzo, but one story from his life shows his greatness as a person.

After winning a tournament, De Vincenzo received his cheque on the eighteenth green, flashed a smile for the cameras, and then walked alone to the clubhouse. As he went to his car, he was approached by a sad-eyed young woman who said to him, 'It's a good day for you, but I have a baby with an incurable disease. It's of the blood and the doctors say she will die.' De Vincenzo paused and then asked, 'May I help your little girl?' He then took out a pen, endorsed his winning cheque and then pressed it into her hand. 'Make some good days for the baby,' he said.

A week later as he was having lunch at a country club, a Professional Golfers Association official approached him, saying, 'Some of the boys in the parking lot told me you met a young woman after you won the tournament.' De Vincenzo nodded. The official said, 'Well, she's a phoney. She has no sick baby. She fleeced you, my friend.'

The golfer looked up and asked, 'You mean that there is no baby who is dying without hope?' This time the PGA official nodded. De Vincenzo grinned and said, 'That's the best news I've heard all week.'

You can easily determine
the calibre of a person by
the amount of opposition it
takes to discourage him.

If you falter in times of trouble,
how small is your strength!
Proverbs 24:10 (NIV)

A student found a cocoon one day and brought it to his biology teacher. She put it in a glass box with a warming lamp. About a week later, the students saw a small opening appear on the cocoon. Then, the cocoon began to shake. Suddenly, tiny antennae emerged, followed by a head and tiny front feet. The students watched the progress of the emerging insect throughout the day. By noon it had freed its listless wings, the colours revealing it to be a monarch butterfly. It wiggled and shook, but try as it might, it could not seem to force its body through the small opening. One student decided to snip off the end of the cocoon to help the insect. Out it plopped. Only the top half of it looked like a butterfly, however. The bottom half was large and swollen. The insect crawled about, dragging its listless wings, and a short time later, it died.

The next day, the biology teacher explained that the butterfly's struggle to get through the tiny opening is necessary in order to force fluids from the swollen body into the wings so they will be strong enough to fly. Without the struggle, the wings never develop.

Struggles cause numerous things in our lives to develop. Rather than struggle *against* struggle, we need to struggle *through* our struggles!

People know what you are by what they see, not by what they hear.

Let your light so shine before men, that they may see your good works and glorify your Father in heaven.
Matthew 5:16 (NKJ)

While doing research for a doctoral thesis, a young man spent a year with a group of Navajo Indians on a reservation in the South West of the USA. He lived with one family, sleeping in their hut, eating their food, working with them and generally living their life.

The grandmother of the family spoke no English, yet a very close friendship formed between her and the doctoral student. They seemed to share the common language of love and they intuitively understood each other. Over the months he learned a few phrases of Navajo, and she picked up words and phrases in English.

When it was time for the young man to return to university and write his thesis, the tribe held a going-away celebration for him. It was marked by sadness since he had developed a close relationship with all those in the village. As he prepared to get into his pick-up truck and drive away, the old grandmother came to say goodbye. With tears streaming from her eyes, she placed her hands on either side of his face, looked directly into his eyes and said, 'I like me best when I'm with you.'

True friendship is letting those around you not only 'be themselves' but 'be their best'.

People who try to whittle you down are only trying to reduce you to their size.

'Blessed are you when men hate you, when they exclude you and insult you and reject your name as evil, because of the Son of Man. Rejoice in that day and leap for joy, because great is your reward in heaven . . .'
Luke 6: 22,23 (NIV)

Japanese bonsai trees are tiny, perfectly formed specimens. Their stature remains small no matter how old a tree gets – most bonsai trees being only fifteen to eighteen inches tall. To make a bonsai tree, a young sapling is first pulled from the soil. Then, its taproot and some of the feeder roots are tied off. Thus, the growth of the bonsai is deliberately stunted.

In sharp contrast, the California sequoia trees grow large. The General Sherman stands 272 feet and measures 79 feet in circumference. If felled, this giant tree would provide enough wood to build 35 five-room homes! The sequoia begins life as a small seed, no larger than the bonsai seed. But its sapling is allowed to be nourished in the rich California soil and sunshine.

Neither the bonsai nor the giant sequoia has a choice in determining how large it will become. But we human beings do! We cannot blame others – including our parents – for what they have done or are doing to us. We have the potential to transplant ourselves into rich, nurturing, positive environments.

If others are trying to whittle you down today, get away from their knife! Rejoice in who you are and who you can be.

Quite often when a man thinks his mind is getting broader, it's only his conscience stretching.

Everything is clean to those who have clean minds. But nothing is wholesome to those who are themselves corrupt and who have no faith in God – their very minds and consciences are diseased.

Titus 1:15 (JBP)

A mother was helping her son one day with his spelling homework and they came to the words *conscious* and *conscience*. She asked her son, 'Do you know the difference between these two words?'

He immediately replied, 'Sure, mum. Conscious is when you are aware of something. And, conscience is when you wish you weren't.'

The conscience is like a sharp square peg in our hearts. When we are confronted by a situation that calls for a right-or-wrong decision, that square begins to turn. Its corners cut into our hearts, warning us with an inward 'knowing' that we are facing a situation in which we must make a choice against evil and for good.

If the conscience is ignored time after time, however, the corners of the square are gradually worn down and it becomes a circle that twists and turns at will. When that circle turns within our hearts, there is no inner sensation of warning. In effect, we are left without a conscience.

A sound conscience is truly a gift from God. Heed its warning signals early and you will be spared much pain and heartache.

Temper is what gets most of us into trouble.
Pride is what keeps us there.

Pride goes before destruction,
a haughty spirit before a fall.
Better to be lowly in spirit and
among the oppressed
than to share plunder with the proud.
Proverbs 16:18,19 (NIV)

In an old monastery near Bebenhausen, Germany, one can see two pairs of deer horns hanging on the wall. The horns are interlocked.

They were found in that position many years ago. Apparently two bucks had been fighting for territorial or herd rights, and their horns became jammed together and could not be separated. They died in a fighting position, unable to find a way of co-operating so that on bended knees, both might eat or drink or eventually be free of the other.

These locked horns are not unlike many relationships that can be found today in homes, schools, factories, offices and even churches. People become entrenched in their positions and angrily confront those who oppose them. In the process, they 'lock horns' and seem unable to ask each other for forgiveness, or find a mutual way of serving one another in love. Both parties in such a relationship suffer, and ultimately lose.

If you are at odds with someone today, go to that person and ask what the two of you might do to reconcile. You may be surprised to find that the other person wants reconciliation as much as you do!

We make a living by what we get – we make a life by what we give.

I have shown you in every way, by labouring like this, that you must support the weak. And remember the words of the Lord Jesus, that He said, 'It is more blessed to give than to receive.'
Acts 20:35 (NKJ)

Two brothers farmed together. They lived in separate houses on the family farm, but met each day in the fields to work together. One brother married and had a large family. The other lived alone. Still they divided the harvest from the fields equally.

One night the single brother thought, *My brother is struggling to support a large family, but I get half the harvest.* With love in his heart, he gathered a box of things he had bought from his earnings – items he knew would help his brother's family. He planned to slip over to his brother's shed, unload the basket there, and never say a word about it.

That same night, the married brother thought, *My brother is alone. He doesn't know the joys of a family.* Out of love, he decided to take over a basket with a quilt and homemade bread and preserves to 'warm' his brother's house. He planned to leave the items on his porch and never say a word.

As the brothers stealthily made their ways to each other's home, they bumped into each other. They were forced to admit to what they were doing and there in the darkness, they cried and embraced, each man realising that his greatest wealth was a brother who respected and loved him.

Our days are identical suitcases – all the same size – but some people can pack more into them than others.

Be very careful, then, how you live – not as unwise but as wise, making the most of every opportunity . . .
Ephesians 5:15,16 (NIV)

Sparky didn't have much going for him. He failed every subject in the eighth grade, and in high school he failed Latin, algebra, English and physics. He made the golf team, but promptly lost the most important match of the season and then lost the consolation match. He was awkward socially – more shy than disliked. He never once asked a girl to go out on a date in high school.

One thing, however, was important to Sparky – drawing. He was proud of his artwork even though no one else appreciated it. He submitted cartoons to the editors of his high school yearbook but they were turned down. Even so, Sparky aspired to be an artist. After high school, he sent samples of his artwork to Walt Disney Studios. Again, he was turned down.

Still, Sparky didn't give up! He decided to write his own autobiography in cartoons. The character he created became famous worldwide – the subject not only of cartoon strips but countless books, television shows and licensing opportunities. Sparky, you see, was Charles Schulz, creator of the 'Peanuts' comic strip. Like his character, Charlie Brown, Schulz may not have been able to do many things. But he made the most of what he *could* do!

Living would be easier if men showed as much patience at home as they do when they're fishing.

You husbands likewise, live with your wives in an understanding way . . .
1 Peter 3:7 (NASB)

Firmin Abautiz was known as a man of serene disposition. Nobody in his town could recall his having lost his temper at any time during his 87 years. One man, who doubted the possibility that a person could be so unflappable, made a deal with the housekeeper, offering her money if she could provoke Abautiz to anger.

The housekeeper knew that Abautiz was very fond of a comfortable, orderly bed, so she neglected to make his bed one day. The next morning, Abautiz kindly pointed it out to her. The next night, Abautiz again found an unmade bed and the following morning, he again called it to her attention. She made a lame excuse, which he kindly accepted.

On the third morning, Abautiz said, 'You still have not made my bed; it is evident you are determined not to do it. Well, I suppose you find the job troublesome; but it is of little consequence, for I begin to be used to it already.' Moved by such goodness of temper, the woman called off the deal and never again failed to make his bed as comfortable as possible!

Not everything can be the way we like it all the time, but criticism and harsh words rarely bring about a lasting and peaceful co-operation or fulfilment of our desires. Patience and kindness on the other hand, do.

Some people succeed
because they are destined to,
but most people succeed
because they are
determined to.

. . . and having done all, to stand. Stand
therefore . . .
Ephesians 6:13,14 (AV)

There once was a Louisville University quarterback who dreamed of playing professional football. Upon graduation, however, no team signed him. So he wrote to several teams and finally got an opportunity to try out for the Pittsburg Steelers. He gave his best effort, but wasn't chosen. His friends said 'You got a raw deal . . . it wasn't meant to be . . . I guess it's time to hang up your boots.' But the young athlete didn't give up. He continued to knock on doors and write letters. Finally, he received another invitation. But again, he didn't make the team.

Most people would have given up long before this point, but not Johnny. He was fanatic about his personal dream. From his early days of playing football with his friends, he had been obsessed with this goal. So, patiently and persistently, he continued to pursue try-out opportunities. Finally, he was invited to try out for the Baltimore team . . . and he made the third string! Through training and many long hours of drills and fitness building, he worked his way up to be starting quarterback. Indeed, he became one of the greatest quarterbacks ever to play in the National Football League. The dreamer's name? Johnny Unitas.

Keep driving until you arrive at your goal line!

God intervenes in the affairs of men by invitation only.

Behold, I stand at the door, and knock: if any man hear my voice, and open the door, I will come in to him, and will sup with him, and he with me.
Revelation 3:20 (AV)

There once was a saintly man who lived on the edge of poverty ... by his own choice. The money he earned, he distributed equally between himself and the poor. The man's adult son was among those who found it extremely difficult to make ends meet, so the man gave him just enough to keep body and soul together, even as he continued to help others who found themselves in dire need. One day the father was asked why he paid so little attention to his son's personal needs while the bulk of his attention went to others. 'You could help your son much more,' his critic said, 'if you would help strangers less.'

'Ah,' the man replied wisely, 'but if I were to meet all my son's requirements, would he perhaps forget the necessity of relying upon the Lord? Would he begin to see me as the source of all his supply, rather than his Heavenly Father? If that became the case, I would not be helping my son at all!'

God forbid that we find ourselves feeling totally self-sufficient, without need. It is in that dark corner that pride lurks. Once pride takes over, we see little reason to invite the Lord to do *His* work in our lives. Take an inventory. Have you invited God into the affairs of your life lately?

The difference between ordinary and extraordinary is that little extra.

Whatever you do, do well, for in death, where you are going, there is no working or planning, or knowing, or understanding.
Ecclesiastes 9:10 (TLB)

Charles E. Kettering, a noted scientist and inventor, believed that the easiest way to overcome defeat was simply to ignore completely the possibility of failure and to keep forging ahead. He once gave an address to Denison University on this theme. He told how he had once given a tough project assignment to a young research worker in a laboratory at General Motors. He wanted to see how the man would react to a difficult problem so he kept from him notes about the project that had been filed in the lab's library. These notes, written by expert researchers, included various sets of statistics and formulas that proved the assignment the young man had been given was impossible to do.

The young research worker set his mind to the project, and worked virtually night and day for weeks. He refused to give up or think the project impossible. One day he came confidently to Kettering to show his work. He had succeeded in doing the impossible!

A little extra time . . . a little extra effort . . . a little extra care . . . a little extra attention sometimes makes all the difference between success and failure, and not only that, but the difference between good and great.

Swallowing angry words is
much better than having to
eat them.

A fool gives full vent to his anger,
but a wise man keeps himself
under control.
Proverbs 29:11 (NIV)

A local newspaper developed a column specifically to interview couples in the town who had reached their golden anniversary of marriage. A brief history of the couple celebrating fifty years of marriage was outlined. Then, the newspaper posed the same question to each spouse: 'To what do you attribute the success of your marriage?' Many of the couples approaching this milestone knew they were going to be interviewed and they gave long thought to the wisest and most practical advice they could give. Some advocated total honesty, others a shared faith, and others abundant communication.

One man lovingly glanced at his wife and then replied: 'The secret of our fifty years of marital harmony is quite simple. My wife and I made an agreement the day we were married. If she was bothered or upset about something, she was to get it off her chest and out in the open. We felt it was important for her to get it out of her system. And, if I was mad at her about something, we agreed I would take a walk. So, I guess you can attribute our marital success to the fact that I have led largely an outdoor life.'

In finding a way to release anger and frustration, make sure your loved ones aren't part of your method!

To forgive is to set a prisoner free and discover the prisoner was YOU.

For if you forgive men when they sin against you, your heavenly Father will also forgive you.
But if you do not forgive men their sins, your Father will not forgive your sins.
Matthew 6:14,15 (NIV)

On February 9, 1960, Adolph Coors III was kidnapped and held for ransom. His body was found seven months later on a remote hillside. He had been shot dead. Adolph Coors IV, who was fifteen years old at the time, lost not only his father but his best friend. For years, young Coors hated Joseph Corbett, the man who was sentenced to life for the murder.

Then in 1975 Ad Coors became a Christian. He knew this hatred for Corbett blighted his growth in faith and also alienated him from other people. Still, resentment seethed within him. He prayed, asking God to help him stop hating Corbett.

Coors eventually felt led to visit Corbett in the maximum security unit of Colorado's Canon City penitentiary. Corbett refused to see him, but Coors left a Bible with this inscription: 'I'm here to see you today and I'm sorry that we could not meet. As a Christian I am summoned by our Lord and Saviour, Jesus Christ, to forgive. I do forgive you, and I ask you to forgive me for the hatred I've held in my heart for you.' Coors later confessed, 'I have a love for that man that only Jesus Christ could have put in my heart.' Coors' heart, imprisoned by hatred, was at last set free.

The company you keep will determine the trouble you meet.

Keep away from angry, short-tempered men, in case you learn to be like them and endanger your soul.
Proverbs 22:24,25 (TLB)

Have you ever seen an entire oyster shell without an oyster in it? You may have wondered, *How did the oyster get out?* You might look for a very small hole in the top of the shell. Such a hole is made by a whelk. This little ocean creature has an appendage that works somewhat like an auger. With it, the whelk bores into the oyster shell and then sucks the oyster through the hole, little by little, until it has devoured it all. Though small, a whelk can do great harm!

Very often, we allow another person's angry outbursts, their critical remarks, or their cynical comments to bore a hole into our good nature and rob us of our otherwise sunny disposition. If we are not careful, we can become irritated to the point where genuine anger and bitterness begin to seethe in us. And when that happens, we are in very real danger of experiencing disease, disharmony and discord.

One of the best things you can do is simply to avoid those people whom you find irksome, continually critical, or habitually angry at life, as well as those who seem to delight in needling you. In other words, stay out of the way of whelks. You'll be happier for it!

Too many parents are not on spanking terms with their children.

He who spares his rod hates his son.
But he who loves him disciplines him
diligently.
Proverbs 13:24 (NASB)

A boy once made headlines as the result of his repeated vandalism in his neighbourhood. Even though he came from a well-to-do family, he was, by every indication of behaviour, a perfect example of a 'juvenile delinquent'. A reporter quizzed the boy in detention, asking, 'Why do you feel the need to destroy property? Are you angry?' The boy just shrugged his shoulders and turned away. The reporter persisted, 'Weren't you afraid of getting a licking from your parents?'

At this the boy looked at the reporter, and said, 'I've never had a licking in my life.' The tone of his voice, however, was not one of anger, but of sadness. The reporter talked with him further and realised that 'not having a licking' meant to this boy that his parents didn't care one whit about him. The young man concluded the interview by declaring that if the police turned him loose, he would continue to take out his vengeance on the neighbourhood until one or other of his parents cared enough to stop him.

Spanking is not nesessarily abuse. Abuse is rooted in a parent's uncontrolled expression of power. Discipline is intended to restrain and re-channel a child's uncontrolled expression of power! Abuse never has a place.

Man cannot discover new oceans unless he has the courage to lose sight of the shore.

'Lord, if it's really you,' said Peter, 'tell me to come to you on the water.'
'Come on, then,' replied Jesus.
Peter stepped down from the boat and began to walk on the water, making for Jesus.
Matthew 14:28,29 (JBP)

Centuries ago, when a mapmaker would run out of the known world before he ran out of parchment, he often would sketch a dragon at the edge of the scroll. This was intended to be a sign to the explorer that he was entering unknown territory at his own risk.

Many explorers, however, did not perceive the dragon as a mapmaker's warning sign, but rather as a prophecy. They foresaw disaster and doom beyond the 'known worlds' they traversed. Their fear kept them from pushing on to discover new lands and peoples.

Other, more adventuresome travellers saw the dragon as a sign of opportunity, the doorway to a new territory worth exploring.

Each of us has a mental map that contains the information we use for guidance as we explore each new day. Like the maps of long ago, our mental maps have edges to them, and sometimes those edges seemed to be marked by dragons, or fears. At times, our fears may be valid. But at other times, our fear may keep us from discovering more of this world, or more about other people – including ourselves. Don't let fear keep you from all that God desires for you to explore and to know!

The heart is the happiest
when it beats for others.

Greater love has no one than this,
than to lay down one's life for his friends.
John 15:13 (NKJ)

One of the people most admired by Charles Swindoll is Dawson Trotman, who died after helping to rescue two drowning girls. Says Swindoll:

'When Dawson Trotman passed away he probably left a legacy of discipleship on this earth that will never be matched except perhaps in the life of Jesus Christ Himself. I've become a real student of Dawson Trotman and believe wholeheartedly in the methods of discipleship that he taught and emulated throughout his days. He died in Schroon Lake, New York. He died of all things in the midst of an area that he was expert in – he drowned. He was an expert swimmer. The last few moments he had in the water he lifted one girl out of the water. He went down and got the other girl and lifted her out of the water and then submerged and was not found again until the dragnet found him a few hours later . . . *Time* ran an article on Trotman's life the next week and they put this caption beneath his name, it read, "Always Holding Somebody Up". In one sentence, that was Trotman's life – investment in people – holding them up.'

Discipleship is not having others follow you as much as it is lifting others up to see the Lord and then serving them so they can follow Him wholeheartedly.

One thing you can learn by watching the clock is that it passes time by keeping its hands busy.

One who is slack in his work
is brother to one who destroys.
Proverbs 18:9 (NIV)

A man was once drawn by the idea that living in 'quiet contemplation away from human society' was the sure path to happiness. He wandered into the desert to become a hermit. After many days, he found a cave near a spring where he could obtain water and grow a few plants for food. Feeling self-sufficient, he spent many idle hours in solitude. Eventually, the hours of the day seemed never to end. His loneliness oppressed him. Feeling more wretched than holy, he cried, 'Father God, let me die. I am weary of this life.' Exhausted, he fell asleep and dreamed that an angel stood before him, saying. 'Cut down the palm tree that grows near the spring and turn its fibres into a rope.'

The hermit awoke and with great effort and many hours of toil, he felled the palm and made a coil of rope from its fibres. Again the angel appeared to him, saying. 'I've seen you smiling every day as you worked. I can tell you are no longer weary of life. Go back into the world with your rope and find employment with it. Let it remind you toil is sweet.'

Work not only benefits the mind and wallet, but the body, emotions and soul. Work keeps all parts of the human machine in order. Just as machines rust out faster than they wear out, so, too, with people.

Now there's even a 'dial-a-prayer' for atheists.
You call a number and nobody answers.

The fool has said in his heart,
'There is no God.'
Psalm 14:1 (NKJ)

The story is told of a colony of mice who made their home at the bottom of a large upright piano. To them, music was frequent, even routine. It filled all the dark spaces with lovely melodies and harmonies.

At first, the mice were impressed by the music. They drew comfort and wonder from the thought that Someone made the music – though invisible to them, yet close to them. They loved to tell stories about the Great Unseen Player whom they could not see.

Then one day an adventuresome mouse climbed up part of the way in the piano and returned with an elaborate explanation about how the music was made. Wires were the secret – tightly stretched wires of various lengths that vibrated and trembled from time to time. A second mouse ventured forth and came back telling of hammers – many hammers dancing and leaping on the wires. The mice decided they must revise their old opinions. The theory they developed was complicated, but complete with evidence. In the end, the mice concluded that they lived in a purely mechanical and mathematical world. The story of the Unseen Player was relegated to mere myth.

But the Unseen Player continued to play nonetheless.

He who thinks by the inch
and talks by the yard
deserves to be kicked
by the foot.

*A fool's lips bring him strife, and his
mouth invites a beating.*
Proverbs 18:6 (NIV)

What must surely be one of the most frustrating conversations in history was reported in *Theatre Arts* magazine. A subscriber, desiring to report on a particular upcoming event in his community, dialled 'Information' to get the magazine's telephone number.

The operator drawled, 'Sorry, but there is nobody listed by the name of 'Theodore Arts'.

The subscriber insisted: 'It's not a person; it's a publication. I want *Theatre Arts.*'

The operator responded, this time a little louder, 'I told you, we have no listing for Theodore Arts in this city. Perhaps he lives in another city.'

By now the subscriber was thoroughly peeved. 'Confound it, the word is Theatre T-H-E-A-T-R-E!'

The operator came back with certainty in her voice. 'That – is not the way to spell Theodore.'

Sometimes there's just no communicating with someone who refuses to hear you, who seems unwilling to understand your point of view, or who simply 'doesn't get' what you are trying to say. Rather than give that person a real kick, however, better to hang up and try dialling someone who can hear you and does understand!

The best inheritance a
father can leave his children
is a good example.

*For you know that we dealt with each
of you as a father deals with his
own children,
encouraging, comforting and urging you
to live lives worthy of God.*
1 Thessalonians 2:11 (NIV)

A young woman relates that when she was a little girl, her father, an artist, would often be busy at his easel, mixing oils and painting on his big canvases while she sat nearby on the floor, working just as hard as he was with her own set of crayons and a colouring book.

Many a time, he would set his brushes aside, reach down, and lift her up onto his lap. Then he'd curl her little hand around one of his brushes, enfolding it with his own larger and stronger hand. And ever so gently, he would guide her hand and the brush, dipping it into the palette and mixing the burnt umbers and raw siennas and then stroke the wet, shiny paint onto the canvas before them both.

The little girl watched in amazement as, together, they made something beautiful.

Little did this father know that he was giving his daughter skills that would bring great fulfilment to her life. Today, Joni Tada – a quadriplegic since a diving accident during her teen years – is still painting, but this time with a paintbrush in her mouth. Much of her earnings is channelled into ministry to help others. Her compassion, too, is a reflection of that shown her by a loving, tender father.

God's Little Devotional Book on Prayer

Our prayers must mean something to us if they are to mean anything to God

Whether you are an uncertain beginner or a confident 'prayer-warrior', you will be continually refreshed and instructed by this insightful prayer companion.

Each double page spread is set out in the form of a daily devotional with a prayer, an extract from Scripture and a reflective passage. Words of wisdom are provided by many Christians – both past and present – such as St Francis of Assissi, John Wesley, John Bunyon, Abraham Lincoln, Billy Graham, Corrie ten Boom, Richard Foster, Walter Wangerin and Charles Swindoll.

Over 300,000 copies sold in the USA in one year!

0 86347 235 4